The Writings of Frithjof Schuon
Series

World Wisdom
The Library of Perennial Philosophy

The Library of Perennial Philosophy is dedicated to the exposition of the timeless Truth underlying the diverse religions. This Truth, often referred to as the *Sophia Perennis*—or Perennial Wisdom—finds its expression in the revealed Scriptures as well as the writings of the great sages and the artistic creations of the traditional worlds.

From the Divine to the Human appears as one of our selections in the Writings of Frithjof Schuon series.

The Writings of Frithjof Schuon

The Writings of Frithjof Schuon form the foundation of our library because he is the pre-eminent exponent of the Perennial Philosophy. His work illuminates this perspective in both an essential and comprehensive manner like none other.

English Language Writings of Frithjof Schuon

Original Books
The Transcendent Unity of Religions
Spiritual Perspectives and Human Facts
Gnosis: Divine Wisdom
Language of the Self
Stations of Wisdom
Understanding Islam
Light on the Ancient Worlds
Treasures of Buddhism (In the Tracks of Buddhism)
Logic and Transcendence
Esoterism as Principle and as Way
Castes and Races
Sufism: Veil and Quintessence
From the Divine to the Human
Christianity/Islam: Essays on Esoteric Ecumenicism
Survey of Metaphysics and Esoterism
In the Face of the Absolute
The Feathered Sun: Plains Indians in Art and Philosophy
To Have a Center
Roots of the Human Condition
Images of Primordial and Mystic Beauty: Paintings by Frithjof Schuon
Echoes of Perennial Wisdom
The Play of Masks
Road to the Heart: Poems
The Transfiguration of Man
The Eye of the Heart
Form and Substance in the Religions
Adastra & Stella Maris: Poems by Frithjof Schuon (bilingual edition)
Autumn Leaves & The Ring: Poems by Frithjof Schuon (bilingual edition)
Songs without Names, Volumes I-VI: Poems by Frithjof Schuon
Songs without Names, Volumes VII-XII: Poems by Frithjof Schuon
World Wheel, Volumes I-III: Poems by Frithjof Schuon
World Wheel, Volumes IV-VII: Poems by Frithjof Schuon
Primordial Meditation: Contemplating the Real

Edited Writings
The Essential Frithjof Schuon, ed. Seyyed Hossein Nasr
Songs for a Spiritual Traveler: Selected Poems (bilingual edition)
René Guénon: Some Observations, ed. William Stoddart
The Fullness of God: Frithjof Schuon on Christianity, ed. James S. Cutsinger
Prayer Fashions Man: Frithjof Schuon on the Spiritual Life, ed. James S. Cutsinger
Art from the Sacred to the Profane: East and West, ed. Catherine Schuon
Splendor of the True: A Frithjof Schuon Reader, ed. James S. Cutsinger

From the Divine to the Human

Survey of Metaphysics and Epistemology

A New Translation with
Selected Letters

by

Frithjof Schuon

Includes Other Previously
Unpublished Writings

Edited by
Patrick Laude

World Wisdom

From the Divine to the Human:
A New Translation with Selected Letters
© 2013 World Wisdom, Inc.

Translated by Mark Perry and Jean-Pierre Lafouge

Published in French as
Du Divin à l'humain:
Tour d'Horizon de Métaphysique et d'Épistémologie
Le Courrier du Livre, 1981

Library of Congress Cataloging-in-Publication Data

Schuon, Frithjof, 1907-1998.
  [Works. Selections. English]
  From the divine to the human : a new translation with selected letters / by
Frithjof Schuon ; edited by Patrick Laude ; translated by Mark Perry and Jean-
Pierre Lafouge.
      pages cm. -- (The writings of Frithjof Schuon)
  "Includes other previously unpublished writings."
  Includes bibliographical references and index.
  ISBN 978-1-936597-32-1 (pbk. : alk. paper) 1. Metaphysics. 2. Knowledge,
Theory of. I. Laude, Patrick, 1958- editor of compilation. II. Perry, Mark, 1951-
translator. III. Lafouge, Jean-Pierre, 1944- translator. IV. Schuon, Frithjof, 1907-
1998. Du divin à l'humain. English. V. Schuon, Frithjof, 1907-1998. Correspond-
ence. Selections. English. VI. Title.
  BD112.S21313 2013
  110--dc23
                                                           2013033691

Cover:
Icon of Pentecost, by Sr. Marie Paul Farran, O.S.B.
© Benedictine Monastery, Mount of Olives, Jerusalem
& Editions Choisir, Geneva,
with permission of the Printery House,
Conception Abbey, Conception, MO 64433, U.S. agent

Printed on acid-free paper in the United States of America

For information address World Wisdom, Inc.
P.O. Box 2682, Bloomington, Indiana 47402-2682
www.worldwisdom.com

CONTENTS

EDITOR'S PREFACE

The original version of the current book, *Du Divin à l'humain*, was arguably the first of Schuon's French language books to focus primarily on metaphysical exposition.[1] Although all of his previous books, beginning with *De l'Unité transcendante des religions* (The Transcendent Unity of Religions) in 1948, are informed by metaphysical principles and contain many pages and insights of a purely metaphysical nature—as Schuon himself indicates when he writes in his foreword: "our position is well known: it is fundamentally that of metaphysics" (p. xi)—it is here that for the first time Schuon explicitly sets forth a survey of pure and universal metaphysics and epistemology. While metaphysics, in the sense of the "science of the universal," as René Guénon has characterized it, remains properly indefinable and inexhaustible, it receives a more "systematic" treatment in *From the Divine to the Human* than in Schuon's previous works.[2]

One of the hallmarks of Schuon's work, here and elsewhere, is his holding fast both to the principle that "God is ineffable" and to the idea that "there are conceptual points of reference which provide a sufficient expression of the nature of God . . . otherwise our intelligence would not be human" (p. 62). Such reference points offer not only a means of intellectual transmission but also of spiritual realization, "for mental formulation contributes to the actualization and assimilation of the immanent lights of the heart" (p. 70).

Related to the above, the publication of the present book inaugurated a sequence of works that manifest a more and more synthetic

---

[1] His first book, written in German, *Leitgedanken zur Urbesinnung* (Guiding Themes for Primordial Meditation), focused on metaphysical exposition as well. It was first published in 1935 with Orell Füssli Verlag in Zürich.

[2] In common with his *Leitgedanken zur Urbesinnung*, Schuon's expression in *From the Divine to the Human* is not primarily tied to any particular religious language—even though *Advaita Vedānta* continues, as in his other French language books, to play a central role in conveying the essentials of the doctrine. In the abovementioned German work even the *Vedānta* is consciously left aside, Schuon having considered his reflections there as "far too primordial to allow of being put in the shadow of a name" (from a letter of 1934, quoted in "Primordial Meditation: Contemplating the Real", trans. Gillian Harris, *Sacred Web*, 20, 2007, p. 20).

and "simple" manner of doctrinal metaphysical exposition—to allude here to the crystalline architectonic unity of this exposition—and that manifest additionally a greater and greater emphasis on the relativity, limitations, and pitfalls of confessional languages when contrasted with the fundamentals of the *religio perennis*, namely, metaphysical discernment, spiritual concentration, and moral conformity. This series of books includes *Sur les traces de la Religion pérenne* (In the Tracks of the Perennial Religion) (1982), *Approches du phénomène religieux* (Insights into the Religious Phenomenon) (1984), and *Résumé de métaphysique intégrale* (Summary of Integral Metaphysics) (1985).[3] It may be noted that, biographically, this series of books coincide with Schuon's move to America in the early 1980s which, according to his biographers, opened a new cycle in his life and creative output.

The title, *From the Divine to the Human*, constitutes in itself an intellectual statement that stands in clear opposition to the trends of modernity and post-modernity. Here it is not the human, but rather the Divine realm that occupies the center and gives meaning to mankind as a theomorphic and "theologic" reality. In this book, which could be regarded as a metaphysical and spiritual *summa*, Frithjof Schuon invites us to a rediscovery of the most profound nature of things, hence of our own Self. Starting from the primary experience of the "miracle of consciousness", he guides us in laying the foundation for the primacy of the Spirit, for the "more" of intelligence cannot derive from the "less" of inert matter. This "blinding evidence", by proving the conformity of human intelligence to its Absolute Object, allows one to explore the mysteries of the Divine so as to shed light, downstream as it were, on the main aspects of human existence, by reason of the unity underlying and linking all that is. This luminous survey "from the Divine to the human" cannot but dissipate the difficulties and troubles that modern mankind often encounters when confronted with the necessary, but sometimes disappointing, exclusivism of revealed religions and the "human margin" that at times obscures them. Thus the way is paved for a spiritual engagement, since one can conclude with the author: "To believe in God is to become

---

[3] All three published by Le Courrier du Livre. The first and last of these French works were included together in the English compilation *Survey of Metaphysics and Esoterism* (1986), while the middle work formed the main part of *In the Face of the Absolute* (1989), both English titles published by World Wisdom.

again what we are; to become it to the very extent that we believe, and that believing becomes being" (p. 130).

The first edition of *Du Divin à l'humain* was published in France in 1981 by Le Courrier du Livre, and was published in an English translation the following year in America by World Wisdom. As in the other recent editions of Schuon's works, this one presents a fully revised translation and includes an appendix, a set of editor's notes, and a glossary. The appendix contains excerpts from Schuon's correspondence and other previously unpublished texts, which prolong, buttress, or develop some of the major ideas presented by Schuon in this book. Although some of these texts were not initially meant to be disseminated to a broader audience, our sense is that, being of a general import and given that "mankind is always mankind"—they can justifiably be included in a printed volume of one of his works. The annotations in the editor's notes are intended to facilitate access to the author's references and allusions as well as to suggest certain cross-relations with passages from his other works; the glossary, for its part, provides translations and definitions of the foreign terms and phrases that the author uses in order to express given metaphysical, cosmological, or spiritual realities with conciseness and precision.[4]

---

[4] In this connection, it should be added that the relative difficulty of Schuon's works is a function of the nature of Reality and not in the least the effect of a conceptual virtuosity or a form of intellectual "art for art's sake". Furthermore, Schuon has himself noted that his works are no "more difficult in [their] approach than the average works of profane philosophy" (p. xi).

FOREWORD

We had no intention of writing a preface for this new book, but we were told that readers unfamiliar with our way of thinking would no doubt wish to know at the outset the underlying doctrine linking subjects that upon first sight appear to be unrelated. Now in fact, they will find this doctrine in this book itself; they will also find it in its most explicit form in some of our preceding works, notably in *Logique et Transcendance, Forme et Substance dans les Religions*, and *L'Esotérisme comme Principe et comme Voie*. We do not believe, moreover, that this present book is more difficult in its approach than the average works of profane philosophy; on the contrary, it seems to us that our way of expressing ourselves, even if at times condensed, as people have remarked, tends to a maximum of clarity and even of simplicity; if difficulties remain, they are to be found in the subject and consequently in the nature of things.

Be that as it may, our position is well known: it is fundamentally that of metaphysics, and this science is by definition universalist, "dogmatist" in the philosophical sense of the term, and traditionalist. It is universalist because free from all denominational formalism; "dogmatist" because far from all subjectivist relativism—we believe that knowledge exists and that it is a real and efficacious adequation; and traditionalist because the religious traditions are there to express, in diverse ways, but unanimously, this quintessential position—at once intellectual and spiritual—which in the final analysis is the reason for being of the human spirit.

Frithjof Schuon, c. 1990

PART 1
SUBJECTIVITY AND KNOWLEDGE

Consequences Resulting from
the Mystery of Subjectivity

The first thing that should strike man when he reflects on the nature of the Universe is the primacy of the miracle of intelligence—or consciousness or subjectivity—whence the incommensurability between it and material objects, whether a grain of sand or the sun, or any creature whatever as an object of the senses. The truth of the Cartesian *cogito ergo sum* is, not that it presents thought as the proof of being, but simply that it enunciates the primacy of thought—hence of consciousness or of intelligence—in relation to the material world surrounding us; certainly, it is not our personal thought that preceded the world, it was—or is—absolute Consciousness, of which our thought is a distant reflection precisely—our thought which reminds us, and proves to us, that in the beginning was the Spirit. Nothing is more absurd than to have intelligence derive from matter, hence the greater from the lesser; the evolutionary leap from matter to intelligence is from every point of view the most inconceivable thing that could be.

We shall no doubt be told that the reality of a creator God has not been demonstrated; however, aside from the fact that it is not difficult to demonstrate this reality with arguments proportionate to its nature—but which for that very reason are inaccessible to certain minds—the least that can be said is that evolution has never been demonstrated by anybody whatsoever, and with good reason; transformist evolution is accepted as a useful and provisional postulate, as one will accept no matter what, provided no obligation is felt to accept the primacy of the Immaterial, since the latter escapes the grasp of our senses. If one starts from the recognition of the immediately tangible mystery that is subjectivity or intelligence, then it is easy to understand that the origin of the Universe is, not inert and unconscious matter but a spiritual Substance which from coagulation to coagulation and from segmentation to segmentation—and other projections both manifesting and limiting—finally produces matter by causing it to emerge from a more subtle substance, but one which is already remote from principial Substance. It will be objected that there is no proof of this, to which we reply—notwithstanding the phenomenon of subjectivity which comprises this proof precisely, and leaving aside other possible intellectual proofs, not needed by Intellection—that there are infinitely fewer proofs for this inconceivable absurdity of evolutionism that makes the miracle of consciousness spring from a pile of earth or stones, metaphorically speaking.

Within the same vein of thought, we shall assert that the ideas of "Great Spirit" and of the primacy of the Invisible are natural to man, something requiring no demonstration; now what is natural to human consciousness, which is distinguished from animal consciousness by its objectivity and its totality—its capacity for the absolute and the infinite, we might say—proves *ipso facto* its essential truth, given that the reason for the existence of intelligence is its adequation to the real.[1] From another point of view, if Intellection and Revelation are "supernaturally natural" to man, their refusal is, quite clearly, also a possibility of human nature otherwise it would not occur; but since man is integrally intelligent, and thereby integrally free, this means by way of consequence that he alone among terrestrial creatures is free to go against his own nature. Now he possesses this liberty only in the wake of a fall which, precisely, separates him first of all from that immanent Revelation which is Intellection, and then sets him against prophetic Revelation which, for its part, compensates for the absence of immanent Science; and which, by this compensation, awakens it, at least in principle.

Extrinsic arguments, as points of reference or as keys, contribute to proving the intellectual and existential primacy of the Spirit, but we have no need of these proofs, be it said once again; if there are people for whom the shadow of a cat does not prove the presence of the real cat, or for whom the sound of a waterfall does not prove the proximity of water, this could not mean that our knowledge of this animal or of this waterfall depends necessarily or exclusively upon the shadow or the sound. Our axiom is that on the one hand all that exists is inscribed *a priori* in the theomorphic substance of our intelligence— there is no integral consciousness that does not prolong absolute Consciousness—and on the other hand that the intellectual actualization of the real or of the possible depends, either on the perfection of our

---

[1] We have heard someone say that the wings of birds prove the existence of air, and that in the same way the religious phenomenon, common *a priori* to all peoples, proves the existence of its content, namely God and the afterlife; which is pertinent if one takes the trouble to examine this point in depth.

nature, or else on an external factor that activates this perfection, or that realizes it if it is partial; a factor such as Revelation or, in a more particular way, such as an experience that provokes the archetypal remembrance of which Plato spoke.

Man's liberty is total, but it cannot be absolute, the quality of absoluteness pertaining solely to the supreme Principle and not to its manifestation, even if it be direct or central. To say that our liberty is total means that it is "relatively absolute", that is to say, it is so on a particular level and within certain limits; nonetheless, our liberty is real—that of an animal is also real in a certain way, otherwise a bird in a cage would not feel itself deprived of freedom—and it is so because liberty as such is liberty and nothing else, whatever its ontological limits may be. As for absolute Liberty, that of the divine Principle, man participates in it to the extent that he conforms to it, and this possibility of communion with Liberty in itself, or with the Absolute, originates precisely from the total, albeit relative, character of our liberty; this amounts to saying that in God and through Him, man can be reunited with pure Liberty; only in God are we absolutely free.

To acknowledge that man is by definition situated between an Intellection which connects him to God and a world which has the power to separate him from God, and that consequently man, being free according to the degree of his intelligence, possesses the paradoxical freedom to wish in his turn to make himself God, is to acknowledge at the same stroke that the possibility of a rupture between Intellection and mere reason is present from the start owing to the very ambiguity of the human condition. The *pontifex* suspended between the Infinite and the finite cannot not be ambiguous, so much so that, inevitably, "offenses must needs come"; it is thus inevitable that man—beginning with the original fall and passing from fall to fall—should end in rationalist luciferianism,[2] which turns against God and thereby opposes itself to our nature; or which turns against our nature and thereby opposes itself to God. The rational faculty, when

---

[2] Or existentialist luciferianism, which on the whole amounts to the same thing, since there is no more argumentative a reasoner than a negator of intellectual efficacy.

separated from its supernatural context, cannot but go against man and is bound to give rise in the end to a way of thinking and a type of life that are contrary to man's nature; in other words: Intellection is not altogether safe except in souls providentially exempted from certain risks inherent in human nature; but it is not—and cannot be—safe in man as such, for the simple reason that man comprises by definition passional individuality, and it is the presence of this individualism, precisely, that creates the risk of a rupture with the pure Intellect, and consequently the risk of the fall.

What is human is what is natural to man, and what is most essentially or most specifically natural to man is that which relates to the Absolute and which therefore requires the transcending of what is earthly in man.[3] And even prior to symbols, doctrines, and rites, our very subjectivity—as we have said—points as clearly as possible to our relationship with the Spirit and the Absolute; were it not for the absolute primacy of the Spirit, relative subjectivity would be neither possible nor conceivable, it would be like an effect without a cause.

Intelligence separated from its supra-individual source is accompanied *ipso facto* by that lack of sense of proportions termed pride; conversely, pride prevents intelligence become rationalism from rising to its source; it can only deny the Spirit and replace it with matter; it is from matter that pride makes consciousness spring forth, or to the extent that it does not succeed in denying it by reducing consciousness to a particularly refined or "evolved" kind of matter—and efforts to do so are not lacking.[4] Rather than to yield to the obvious fact of the Spirit, proud reason will deny its own nature which nonethe-

---

[3] The word "humanism" constitutes a curious abuse of language in view of the fact that it expresses a notion contrary to the integrally human, hence to the human properly so called: indeed, nothing is more fundamentally inhuman than the "purely human", namely the illusion of constructing a perfect man starting from the individual and the terrestrial; whereas the human in the ideal sense draws its reason for being and its entire content from that which transcends the individual and the earthly.

[4] Whether one speaks of "energy" rather than "matter"—and other subtleties of the kind—changes nothing with respect to the crux of the problem and merely adds to the complexity of the difficulty. Let us mention that a so-called "socio-biologist"—this word is an entire program unto itself—has carried ingenuity to the point of replacing matter with "genes", whose blind egoism, combined with an instinct belonging to ants or bees, somehow ended up forming not only bodies but also consciousness and finally human intelligence, the latter being miraculously capable of discoursing intelligently on the very genes that amused themselves in producing it in the first place.

less enables it to think; however, in its concrete conclusions, it lacks imagination and a sense of proportions as much as it does intellectual perspicacity, and this is precisely a consequence of its pride. *Corruptio optimi pessima*: it is this that proves, once again, the monstrous disproportion between the cleverness of reason turned luciferian and the falseness of its results; tons of intelligence are wasted to circumvent the essential while brilliantly proving the absurd, namely to prove that the spirit sprung in the end from a clod of earth—or, we could say, from an inert substance—over the course of billions of years, the quantity of which, with respect to the supposed result, is ridiculous and proves nothing. There is a loss of common sense here and a perversion of the imagination that, strictly speaking, no longer have anything human about them, a loss that can only be explained by the well-known scientistic prejudice that seeks to explain everything from below; to erect no matter what hypothesis, provided it excludes real causes, which are transcendent and not material, and whose concrete and tangible proof, finally, is our subjectivity.

Spirit is Substance, matter is accident: in other words, matter is but a contingent and transitory modality of the radiation of the Spirit that projects the worlds and the cycles while remaining transcendent and immutable. This radiation produces the polarization into subject and object: matter is the terminal point of descent of the objective pole, sensorial consciousness being the subjective phenomenon that corresponds to it. The object for the senses is matter, or shall we say the perceptible physical domain; for the Intellect, objective reality is the Spirit in all its forms. It is by it that we exist, and that we know; were it not immanent in physical substances, these could not exist for a single instant. And in this Spirit, precisely, the subject-object opposition is resolved; it is resolved in Unity which is at once exclusive and inclusive, transcendent and immanent. The alpha as well as the omega, although transcending us infinitely, reside in the depths of our heart.[5]

---

[5] The key to the Delphic mysteries is: "Know thyself" (*Gnothi seauton*); to know the nature of subjectivity is to know the structure of the world.

That which we can and must know, that we are; and this is why we can know it, infallibly, provided we are liberated from the veils which separate us from our true nature. Man imposes these veils upon himself because his luciferian will identifies itself with them; or because he believes that he recognizes himself in them; and therefore to remove them is to die. That at least is what man feels so long as he has not understood that "I am black, but beautiful".

There are moreover, in favor of the primacy of the Spirit, extrinsic proofs that are hardly insignificant; we have often alluded to them, and they result from the very nature of man. If everything has begun with matter, and if there is no Spirit, and thus no God, how can we explain that men were able firmly to believe the contrary for thousands of years, and that they even expended a maximum of intelligence in affirming it and a maximum of heroism in living up to it. One cannot lay claim to progress, since the unbelievers of every kind are far from being superior to believers and sages, and nowhere does one see an evolutionary transition from the latter to the former; materialistic ideas have manifested and spread, so to speak, before our eyes—since the "Age of Enlightenment"—without it being possible to note therein an evolution in the direction of a qualitative ascent, both intellectual and moral, quite to the contrary.

Those who uphold the evolutionist argument of an intellectual progress are fond of explaining religious and metaphysical ideas in terms of inferior psychological factors, such as fear of the unknown, childish hope of a perpetual happiness, attachment to an imagery that has become dear, escape into dreams, the desire to oppress others at small expense, *et cetera*; how can one fail to see that such suspicions, shamelessly presented as proven facts, contain psychological inconsistencies and impossibilities, which cannot escape any impartial observer? If humanity has been stupid for thousands of years, one cannot explain how it could have ceased being so, all the more as this change occurred in a very short period of time; and one can explain it still less when one observes with what intelligence and heroism it has been stupid for so long and with what philosophic myopia and moral decadence it finally became "lucid" and "adult".[6]

---

[6] A characteristic trait of "our times" is that everywhere "the cart is put before the horse": that which normally should be the means, becomes the end, and inversely. Machines are supposed to be there for men, but in fact men are there for the machines;

The essence of the real is the banal or the trivial, scientists and other pseudo-realists seem to be saying. To which we could answer: the essence of the real is the miraculous; the miracle of consciousness, of intelligence, and of knowledge. In the beginning was, not matter, but Spirit, which is the Alpha and the Omega.

whereas formerly roads were there for the towns, now the towns are there for the roads; instead of mass media being there for "culture", the latter is there for the mass media, and so forth. The modern world is an inextricable tangle of revolvings that no one can stop.

Aspects of the Theophanic
Phenomenon of Consciousness

The characteristics that man shares with animals are not by definition beneath man and unworthy of him; they become so only when man renounces his humanity and fails to humanize what he shares with animals. Now to humanize is to spiritualize, or to sacralize; it is to open the natural to the supernatural, from which it proceeds ontologically; it is to make the natural element the support for an awareness of the supernatural. For man, earthly experience coincides with the remembrance of a Paradise which, though lost, is still there, beneath the surface, and capable of being actualized.

What animals and man have in common is, first of all, sensorial and instinctual intelligence; then the faculties of the senses, and finally basic feelings. What is proper to man alone is the Intellect open to the Absolute; and also, owing to that very fact, reason, which extends the Intellect in the direction of relativity; and consequently it is the capacity for integral knowledge, for sacralization, and for ascension. Man shares with animals the wonder of subjectivity—but strangely a wonder that is not understood by the evolutionists; however, the subjectivity of animals is only partial, whereas that of man is total; the sense of the Absolute coincides with totality of intelligence.

The Intellect, the mental faculties, and the sensorial faculties, including sexual sensibility, are all so many aspects of this "naturally supernatural" wonder that is subjectivity. And this subjectivity comprises two summits or two scales, one intellectual and one vital: intellective union and carnal union; the second is typically defined as being "animal", which, of course, makes sense only on condition of removing from the idea of animality its pejorative connotation and making it neutral like the ideas of life and consciousness.[1] In reality, what we share with animals is both animal and human; sexuality, for instance, is animal in animals and human in men. To say that it is

[1] It is curious to note that it is precisely these two scales, intellective union and sexual union, that a certain religious moralism holds in suspicion or condemns, as the case may be, which indicates a contrario the paradoxical but real connection between the summits of intelligence and of life.

human means in practice that it requires spiritualization, hence inte-riorization and sacramentalization; human sexuality is specifically and pejoratively animal when man wishes it so, but not in the framework of what is truly human, which is spiritual.[2]

There is, moreover, a kind of compensatory complementarity between intellection and orgasm: just as sexual union, in order to be properly human, demands its sacramentalization and its spiritualiza-tion and hence its interiorization, so likewise—but conversely—intellectual knowledge, which is first of all mental and theoretical, demands a concretization in depth which adds an ecstatic dimension to it, whence the association of ideas between wisdom and wine.[3] Let us recall in this connection that the Heart-Intellect is the seat not only of Knowledge but also of Love, that it is both Light and Heat; there is in fact no complete knowledge without the concurrence of the ele-ment love or beauty, any more than there is perfect love without the concurrence of the element knowledge or truth.

Even so, it would be perfectly false to conclude, from what has just been said, that intellectuality needs sexuality as the latter needs intellectuality or spirituality; what the human spirit needs is not the sexual element, it is the element of infinitude of which sexuality is the manifestation on the vital and psychic plane. While intellectuality or spirituality comprises a supernatural element by definition—a permanent or incidental intervention of the Holy Spirit—sexuality is something simply natural: but since it reflects a divine reality, it becomes a quasi-sacramental support for that experience of infinitude which is contemplative extinction;[4] we could also say that it becomes so because it is human, and is for that reason intended for a spiritual purpose as well. All this evokes by analogy the alchemy proper to

[2] The sexual question is a thorny one in a Christian climate because the Christian be-liever finds it difficult to understand that this subject can be broached without one's having a personal interest in it; this obliges us to specify, for all intents and purposes, that we are speaking of it because the nature of things prompts us to do so and not in order to defend a particular cause or other; given that our vocation is spirituality, all that is human is ours.

[3] *In vino veritas*, says an ancient proverb recorded by Alcaeus; in the same sense, The-ocritus brings out the esoteric connection between "intoxication" and "truth".

[4] As Ibn Arabi, notably, pointed out; but even the cult of the Lady among the knights and troubadours, or the *Fedeli d'Amore* would have no meaning outside of this analogy which is both doctrinal and alchemical or, one might say, "Tantric".

sacred art: this art, as we have said more than once, transmits not only abstract truths conveyed by symbolism, it also transmits, by its very beauty, the perfumes at once vivifying and appeasing of divine Love.[5]

There can be a spiritualization of sexuality just as conversely there can be an animalization of intelligence; in the first case, what can be the occasion of a fall becomes a means of elevation; in the second case, intelligence is dehumanized and gives rise to materialism, even existentialism, hence to a "thinking" that is human only by its mode, but whose content is properly sub-human. The flagrant contradiction of materialism is the negation of the spirit by means of the spirit; and that of existentialism is to use this negation as the basis for dismantling the normal functions of intelligence under the pretext of defending the rights of "existence" or of the "concrete" against "abstraction". "The more he blasphemes, the more he praises God", says Eckhart; materialist and concretist ideologies, by the very excess of their inanity, bear witness indirectly to the reality of the spirit and consequently also to its primacy.[6]

All of these considerations are linked with what we have said before on the phenomenon of subjectivity, in that this phenomenon proves by its mere existence the inanity of the evolutionist and transformist thesis. Just as neither consciousness nor *a fortiori* intelligence can spring forth from "matter"—however matter may be explained—neither can that modality of consciousness which is love be derived from

---

[5] The Prophet of Islam teaches not only that "God is beautiful and loveth beauty" but also that "beauty of character is half of the religion"; this means that the sense of beauty is nothing unless it coincides with the sense of the sacred and with moral nobility. Let us take note that, according to another *hadīth*, "marriage is half of the religion" which, in the light of the preceding *hadīth*, indicates how the role of marriage is a means of forming character.

[6] The existentialist will not ask, "What is this thing?" but "What does this thing mean for me?" Thus he will put the entirely subjective "meaning" in place of the objective nature, which is not only the height of absurdity but also of pride and insolence. Given that true greatness "means" nothing for the little man, he will see in it only a kind of infirmity the better to be able to savor his own "meaningful" inflatedness.

it, always for the simple reason that the greater cannot come from the lesser; and it is a question here of an infinitely greater.

One must not tire of affirming this: the origin of a creature is not a material substance, it is a perfect and non-material archetype: perfect, therefore without any need of a transformative evolution; non-material, therefore having its origin in the Spirit, not in matter. Assuredly, there is a trajectory; but this starts not from an inert and unconscious substance,[7] it proceeds from the Spirit—the womb of all possibilities—to the earthly result, the creature; and this result issued from the invisible at a cyclic moment when the physical world was still far less separate from the psychic world than in later and pro-gressively more "hardened" periods. When one speaks traditionally of *creatio ex nihilo*, what is meant, on the one hand, is that creatures do not derive from a pre-existing matter and, on the other, that the "incarnation" of possibilities cannot in any way affect the immutable Plenitude of the Principle.

In the beginning was the Spirit: hence the Word; for the Spirit, wanting and having to impart itself because It is the Sovereign Good, brings about the manifestation of Its innumerable possibilities. The Spirit is at once Light and Heat; now when we consider them on the plane of their earthly manifestation, heat, which is life, is as miracu-lous as light, which is intelligence. Be that as it may, to reduce all intelligence and all love to material causes is a way of not wanting to admit that our material existence is an exile; it is, on the contrary, to want to feel at ease in a world that appears as an end in itself, and which exempts man from the effort of transcending things and of transcending himself; when in fact without this effort man falls short of the human vocation.

If the evolutionists are right, the human phenomenon cannot be accounted for properly and human life is not worth living. These are moreover the conclusions they reach in the end, whence their axiom of the absurdity of existence; in other words, evolutionists attribute to the object, which is inaccessible to them, the absurdity of the subject, which they have deliberately chosen by following downwards not innocent animality but human animality.

---

[7] Whether one fancies it is charged with evolutive "energy", or whether one transforms it into "genes" or into whatever else one pleases, changes nothing to the question.

Credo ut intelligam; if, on the one hand, this saying expresses the viewpoint of a voluntarist spirituality, on the other hand it bears witness to the fact that believing is a way of understanding by virtue of a foreknowledge which is "supernaturally natural" to man, to the very measure that he consents to remain faithful to his nature and to his vocation.

Transcendence Is Not Contrary to Sense

To speak of human knowledge is to speak of knowledge of the Absolute; and this latter knowledge evokes the mystery of the degrees of reality, hence the mystery of relativity, not only the relativity of the world but also—and *a priori*—that of the personal aspect of the Divinity. It is here that certain difficulties—either conceptual or dialectical—occur: on the one hand there is the metaphysical need to acknowledge this mystery, and on the other hand there is the theological impossibility of acknowledging it without at the same time, if not of negating it explicitly, at least of leaving it unaddressed; speaking very schematically, it is as if, being obliged to admit the existence of concentric circles, one hastened to add that they are radii, in order to safeguard the homogeneity of the system, and because of a prejudice favoring linear continuity, or favoring unity in spite of everything.[1] This is to say that dogmatist speculation is unaware of that inward mobility that, in other disciplines, allows for different perspectives to be situated hierarchically without sacrificing any of them, and without abusively reducing any single one of them to another.

Within relativity there is with respect to the Absolute a relationship of radiation, extension, or continuity, and a relationship of reflection, repetition, or discontinuity: to affirm that the hypostases do not in any way pertain to the first relationship would amount to denying their divine character—illustrated by geometric continuity—for then only the Essence would be divine, the geometric point alone being central; to affirm, on the contrary, that the hypostases, although relative,[2] do not in any way pertain to the second relationship would amount to denying their separation from the pure Absolute, for then they would be the Essence and the Essence would be differentiated—

[1] This difficulty moreover brings to mind the classic misunderstanding between Semitic monotheism and Aryan, or other, polytheism. In fact, there is no polytheism properly so-called, except perhaps subjectively—*de facto* and not *de jure*—in the case of a popular degeneration which we would term "pagan".

[2] In the sense—paradoxical but real—of the "relatively absolute": hypostases are relative with respect to the Essence, but they are principial—hence in practice absolute—with respect to cosmic Manifestation.

hence affected by relativity—which is a contradiction in terms. There are also, still within relativity, the relationships of difference and of identity: one hypostasis is distinct from another on pain of being the other and not itself, but it is identical to the other with respect to principial substance, thus to its divine character. This dimension of distinction and indistinction which is, so to speak, "horizontal", causes no difficulty; however, such is not the case with the "vertical" dimension of continuity and discontinuity, for here a question of "sublimeness" enters into play, and this is something to which religious sentiment is particularly sensitive, not to mention the care taken to avoid the risks of heresy: in other words, it is necessary at all costs to avoid, on the one hand, placing one or several gods alongside God and, on the other hand, introducing into God a scission, which would amount more or less to the same thing; the divine Nature has to remain simple, just as the divine Reality has to remain one, notwithstanding the undeniable complexity of the divine Mystery.

Without this complexity there would be no world; to deny it would amount to maintaining that the Absolute is deprived of the dimension of Infinitude. And if God were not essentially simple, Reality would not be one; there would be several Existences producing existent things, which is contradictory, hence absurd, Existence being unique by definition.

On the one hand God is absolute, and on the other hand He can be differentiated; but He cannot be so on the same plane or in the same respect. If He is absolute, it is because He transcends his differentiated aspects, such as the Trinity, creative Power, Omniscience, Omnipotence; if He is differentiated or qualified—which amounts to the same thing—it is because He is envisaged in a way that is already relative, even though this aspect is absolute with regard to creatures as such, since it is principial as is the entire divine order.[3]

---

[3] For Meister Eckhart, the "ground" of the soul transcends the soul, as the "Godhead" (*diu Gotheit*) transcends the "God" (*Got*) of the Three Persons. In speaking of Beyond-Being—for the "uncreated" essence of the Intellect has access thereto, and that is the perspective of immanence—and in comparing this mystery to a little "fortress" (*daz*

Now according to the objection of certain believers, who seek to reduce metaphysics to their creed, "God" would be the Absolute in every respect; the logic of the metaphysician, which cannot accept this equation, would not be applicable to God; the idea that the divine qualities and the personal character of God pertain to relativity would not be theological or pneumatological, but merely logical, which would prove the incompetence of human intelligence in this matter; God would not be subject to the laws of reason, and to believe the contrary would be a luciferian perversion.[4] We could respond with good reason—since it has come to that—that it is the reverse which is a perversion of the human spirit: that is to say, to believe that the nature of God must appear as absurd to human intelligence; to believe, in other words, that God, after having given us intelligence—not "logic" alone—could require us to admit what is contrary to this gift; or to believe that God could have given us an intelligence contrary to the most lofty contents of which it is capable and for which it is made; thus, that He could have given us an intelligence inoperative with respect to truths concerning it, whereas it is precisely human—not animal—intelligence which is "made in the image of God" and which determines the rest of the human phenomenon, from its vertical posture to its gift of language. Someone has claimed that the laws of reason or of logic are not rooted in God, or if they are, that they are so just as everything else is, due to the mere fact that they exist; in which case, it would be pointless to proclaim that God made man in his image. If no matter what is made in the image of God—in the direct sense intended by Scripture—then it is pointless to speak of

bürgelīn), Eckhart specifies that "God himself never casts a single glance therein (*luoget dā niemer in*) . . . inasmuch as He possesses the modes and properties of his Persons. . . . When He is the absolutely simple One, without any mode or any property: He is not there in the sense of Father, Son, or Holy Spirit, but He is nonetheless a Something (*ein waz*) which is neither this nor that" (first of the sermons beginning with the citation: *Intravit Jesus in quoddam castellum*). Again according to Eckhart, "all that is in the Deity is one, and of that Godhead there is no occasion to speak. God acts, the Godhead acts not at all. . . . God and Godhead differ by acting and non-acting" (Sermon *Nolite timere eos. . .*).

[4] This temptation is not peculiar to Christianity, it occurs almost inevitably in all exoteric ambiences. Ashari, for example, deems that God has the "right" to be unjust and that it is man who sees things in a distorted manner; he forgets that if such were the case, "the Just" (*Al-Hakīm*) would not be a divine Name and man would not be deiform.

human theomorphism; if, on the contrary, there is theomorphism, it must concern above all the intelligence, which is the essence and the very reason for being of man.

In reality, the laws of intelligence, hence also those of reason, reflect the laws of the divine Intellect; they cannot be contrary to it. If the functions of intelligence were opposed to the nature of God, then there would be no need to speak of intelligence, precisely; intelligence, by definition, must be fitted to the knowable, which means at the same time that it must reflect the divine Intelligence, and this is why man is said to be "made in the image of God". It is said nowadays that Plato, Aristotle, and the Scholastics are "outdated"; this means, in reality, that there is no longer anyone intelligent or normal enough to understand them, the height of originality and emancipation being to mock things which should normally be obvious.

But, to return to those fideists who scorn intelligence: what then, we ask, are the mysterious defects inherent in thinking and contrary to the fundamental facts of the divine nature, and what would be the reason for the existence of these defects? If already man is made to know God, and if therefore God requires of him that he know Him, how can one explain—repeating here our argument made earlier—that God could have endowed man with an instrument of perception which provides what is contrary to reality, or provides it in an arbitrary manner beyond a certain level? For it is obvious that if certain philosophers deny God—those precisely who detach reason from its roots—it is not because reason obliges them to do so, otherwise atheism would be natural to man,[5] and otherwise a Plato or an Aristotle would not have taken the trouble to speak of God, though they are still accused of rationalism; the very structure of reason would have dispensed them from doing so. Of course, these arguments could not be addressed to those theologians who admit—and such is the norm—that "sacred science" is not contrary to reason; it is addressed to those—be they theologians or not—who consider that Revelation can claim the right to clash head-on with even the most well-endowed, the most well-informed, and the most well-meaning of intelligences, without offering them anything more than Pascal's wager.

---

[5] Which is amply belied by experience. There is no people on earth which is not religious *a priori*.

To the extent that God makes Himself the object of our intelligence, it is He Himself who knows Himself in us; and the rational faculty, whether capable of grasping all the dimensions of this knowledge or not, is at least conformed, by its structure and its functions, to this knowledge.

When it is said, traditionally, that reason cannot attain to God, what must be understood is this: reason by itself, hence deprived of necessary information and cut off from its intuitive root, namely the Intellect; but this could not mean that reason is constituted—through a caprice of the Creator (*quod absit*)—to make that which is divinely true appear as logically contradictory, hence absurd. Certainly, reason cannot convey the Inexpressible; but conversely, nothing that is expressible could in itself be contrary to reason. A given metaphysical expression may be accidentally illogical, but then that is due either to our ignorance of certain data, or to the elliptical character of the expression.[6]

Man is distinguished from animals by the totality—hence the objectivity—of his intelligence, and the sign of this totality is not only the rational faculty, but also language; now the domain of language is that of logic, so much so that logic concerns all that is expressible. Consequently, let no one come and tell us that there is something in the expressible which escapes logic and which has the right to abolish it; no religion imposes this opinion upon us; and never has any religion warned us that our intelligence, or our faculty of thought, comprises inherent defects that place it in contradiction with what religion asks us to believe. If someone asks us to admit this postulate which is, to say the least, aberrant, we certainly have no reason for doing so; what motive would we have for believing, on a plane which does not escape our thought empirically in any way, that our intelligence no longer functions? If an idea is not compelling either by its evidence or even by its plausibility, if it is in every respect unintelligible, on what grounds would it be compelling for us, and what motive would we

---

[6] Which is to say that in such a case there is apparent or extrinsic, not real and intrinsic, absurdity.

have for believing it is true? Is it with the intelligence that we should admit that intelligence is intrinsically incompatible with the knowledge of God?

Believers who oppose reason—and possibly intelligence as such—convince themselves that the human mind is capable of logic only; in other words, they deny Intellection, and they do so, according to them, for the sake of Revelation. They of course make retrospective use of logical arguments, and deny that they reject logic in itself; but instead of understanding that the logic of the pure metaphysician—of the Platonic or Vedantic type—is also retrospective, and that it is so with respect to Intellection,[7] precisely, they reduce the theses of the metaphysician to the logic that he uses to express himself, and they do so while claiming for themselves the right to present supra-rational certitudes logically; two standards, two sets of rules.

To the detractors of logic on the plane of sacred epistemology, we could provisionally ask the following question: who ever obliged Gregory Palamas to imagine something like the divine "Energies", were it not the logical necessity of building a bridge between his *deus absconditus* and the world?[8] We say "imagine" because this concept of "Energies" has no scriptural or patristic foundation—unless one really wanted to press the point, which is all too easy to do—yet at the same time we ask this question in a "provisional" manner, because we are quite willing to admit that Gregory Palamas followed an intellectual intuition, or let us say an "inspiration" of the Holy Spirit;[9] but then no one should accuse the Platonists of always having been fooled by an

---

[7] Principial or rational retrospectivity, of course, and not temporal.

[8] The "Byzantine" controversy on the unknowability of God is rather intriguing: is He unknowable due to a deficiency in our mind, or is He so due to His very nature? Both theses are at once true or false according to the relationships in view.

[9] The distinction between the Essence and the Energies might well be equivalent to that between Beyond-Being and Being, but the question which arises here is that of knowing to what degree one draws the consequences implied in the two notions, or rather, to what degree one perceives the scope of the two principles. In general, theological doctrines do not adopt this point of view, mindful as they are to have the one and total Divinity enter into each of the divine aspects, in order to forestall the danger of heresy, and this at the risk of shattering the formulations, that is to say of giving them a paradoxical and at the very least a problematical character. This, precisely, has led some people to hold that the divine Truth has the "right" to be absurd, not for the way of thinking of rationalists only, but for human reason as such.

altogether artificial logic, and no one should extend this reproach to all non-Christian sages. It is easy to see why in the one case logic is meant to serve as a vehicle for aid from Heaven, whereas in the other case it is accused of being a human machination: this is because denominational begging of the question forbids accepting as valid what has not been issued from a given religious clique.

We will be told that the divine nature is not subject to the laws of logic. No doubt; but the laws of logic are ontologically subject to divine nature, to which they indeed bear witness; and this is altogether different. And if there are sectors wherein the laws of logic become practically inoperative, without thereby being contradicted, intelligence understands why it is so; it knows that the formal cannot express the non-formal exhaustively, and this awareness is far from being illogical. Someone might mention, so as to confound our rationality, the virgin birth of Christ or the real presence in the Eucharist, or the resurrecting of the dead, or some miracle or other; but these things are perfectly in conformity to logic when one knows their nature. Divine Omnipotence means that God can do anything in the phenomenal order, but it cannot mean that God be at one and the same time and in the selfsame relationship both absolute and relative, simple and differentiated; God can do anything, but He cannot be contrary to His nature; He cannot not be God.

—— ·÷· ——

The monotheistic religions represent ways of salvation—upheld by a morality and a mysticism—but not expressly metaphysical doctrines; at least this is so when we envisage them—as they require *a priori*—in their literal and immediate meaning which alone compels recognition as a *conditio sine qua non*; but since religion necessarily comprises a character of totality—its requirement of total adherence indicates this—it has to offer total truth, hence pure metaphysics, albeit in an indirect and implicit manner. It offers this, not in the literal articulation of its dogmas, but in their symbolism, which by definition is universal; thus, when the Fathers of the Church declare that "God became man, in order that man might become God", there is to be found therein a significance that transcends the literal meaning of voluntarist and individualist redemptionism. The entire doctrine of the

Word constitutes a system of points of reference at the level of the one metaphysics, and in this sense it is possible to speak of a metaphysics that is Christian in its formulation; but what one cannot do is to claim that there exists an explicit metaphysics and an epistemology incumbent upon all Christians and that are contrary to all the other doctrines of the same kind.

Thus if the metaphysician of Christian persuasion concurs with the dogmas, it is because he perceives their universal truth and not because he intends to reduce the Absolute to a given relative aspect of the Real; however, it is false to contest the unanimity of metaphysics by arguing that doctrines are diverse, for this diversity in no way prevents the essential truths from being of dazzling unanimity.

But let us return to the problem of the absolute and non-absolute aspects of the divine Principle: never has Scripture declared that the Father, the Son, and the Holy Ghost—or that the "Lord of hosts" of the Old Testament—constitute the Absolute.[10] The Christian creed requires belief "in God, the all-powerful Father, creator of heaven and earth", and not the belief that God is the Absolute; certainly, it is necessary to believe that nothing is above God, but the divine Essence is not, precisely, another God above the differentiated and acting God; it is the same God, but envisaged in another respect, or rather outside of all determinative and limitative relationships.[11]

---

[10] Given that metaphysics is not the property of any one denomination, we see diverse doctrinal accentuations at the heart of every religion; it is neither Christianity nor Islam which commands or forbids our being inspired by Plato rather than Aristotle, or conversely.

[11] Concerning the transcendence of Beyond-Being, it is necessary to emphasize that in reality it is absolute plenitude and cannot therefore have a privative meaning: to say that the Trinity is surpassed therein means, not that it is abolished as regards what is essential to it, but that it is comprised—and prefigured with respect to its ontological or hypostatic projection—in Beyond-Being in a manner at once undifferentiated and eminently positive; it is so in the manner of the Vedantic *Sat-Chit-Ānanda* which, while corresponding to an already relative vision, is nonetheless comprised in an ineffable and super-eminent manner in the pure absoluteness of *Ātmā*.

The importance of this idea of the degrees of the Real rests on the fact that this idea indicates the totality of knowledge. In Hinduism, this totality is represented by Shankara, as is well known, whereas for Ramanuja, just as for the Semitic exoterisms, the Real does not comprise extinctive degrees; among the Greeks, we encounter the awareness of these degrees in Platonic idealism, but scarcely so in Aristotelian hylomorphism, which accentuates or favors the "horizontal" perspective; whence its utility for scientism on the one hand, and for a theology more cosmological than metaphysical on the other hand; science being centered on the world, and religion on the eschatological interests of man.

Knowledge of the Absolute, which coincides in principle with the plenitude of intelligence, implies knowledge of the relative, hence also of the illusory nature of the latter; nothing can oblige us to admit that a given relative reality is absolute—namely to admit it for the simple reason that it is sublime or because dogma does not specify its ontological relativity. We have just said that knowledge of the Absolute coincides "in principle" with total intelligence: this reservation means that man does not have the right to lay claim to transcendent truths except in proportion to his sincerity, and that he proves this sincerity by the consequences he draws from these truths on the individual plane; otherwise he is simply "as sounding brass or a tinkling cymbal". There is no intellectual extra-territoriality on the integrally human plane in this case; our "knowing" must harmonize with our "being", and conversely.

There are two tendencies in the human spirit, either to reduce God to the world or the Absolute to the relative, or to reduce the world to God or the relative to the Absolute; now quite clearly the second tendency implies the idea of the degrees of the Real, whereas the first is averse to it and embraces everything in one and the same "existence". There are those who in practice reduce God to the world while maintaining within this framework the idea of transcendence; the others, and rightly so, reduce cosmic manifestation to the divine Principle, while specifying *a priori* the nothingness of all manifestation before the Principle.

In Christian language, we would say that the Incarnation—the fact that "God became man"—proves the principially divine nature of the Intellect, and excludes that any modality of intelligence—notably reason—be affected with defects incompatible with the nature of

God.[12] The laws of logic are sacred, for they pertain essentially to ontology, which they apply to a particular domain; logic is so to speak the ontology of that microcosm which is human reason. The transcendent prototype of reason is Being which measures and coordinates its possibilities, just as the transcendent prototype of the Intellect is the divine Consciousness turned towards its undifferentiated Infinitude; man is logical because God is and because, precisely, God created him "in His image". But "like God", man is not merely logical, he is also artist, poet, musician; necessity is combined with freedom.

We do not say that something is true because it is logical, we say that it is logical because it is true; we perceive a given truth beyond logic since we have the intuition of it intellectually—Intellection being a kind of seeing and not a conclusion—but it is necessary for us to refer to logic as soon as we wish to explain something, unless we express ourselves by means of a symbol, but the symbol is a suggestion aiming at intuition, not an explanation addressing itself to thought.

No doubt, it happens that there are flagrant contradictions in logic within the sacred Scriptures and within the writings of sages, but these contradictions and inconsistencies are only apparent and derive simply from the elliptical character of the expression, as we have remarked above. It is a question then of an allusive dialectic addressing intuition and intellectual imagination; and it is the role of commentators to restore to the formulations the missing links and thus to reveal the intention of the author. Be that as it may, possible alogicality is not necessary illogicality; there is no sacred right to absurdity.

It is not for nothing that "logic" (*logikos*) comes from "Logos", which derivation indicates, in a symbolical fashion at least, that logic—the mental reflection of ontology—cannot, in its substance, derive from human arbitrariness; that, on the contrary, it is a quasi-

---

[12] If the Message of Christ—which is *a priori* a way of salvation for everyone and not a sapiential doctrine—is "folly in the eyes of the world", this is, not because it would imply a contradiction, *quod absit*, but because the world follows a way contrary to this Message, while referring possibly to inoperative philosophies or to philosophies become inoperative.

pneumatological phenomenon in the sense that it results from the divine Nature itself, in a manner analogous—if not identical—to that of intellectual intuition. It is necessary to insert here the notion of the "naturally supernatural", which possibility is situated as it were between the natural pure and simple and the miraculous, and which for this very reason is specifically human, since man is *pontifex*. Nature and super-nature, fallibility and infallibility; now this last element, which pertains to super-nature, is "incarnated" in nature as well, by introducing into it a supernatural character, precisely.

In summary: let us admit that human logic is at times inoperative; however, it is not inoperative because it is logical, but because it is human; because, being human, it is subject to psychological and material contingencies which prevent it from being what it is in itself, and what it is by its origin and in its source, where it coincides with the being of things.

As is proved by the practice of meditation, intuition can arise as the result of a rational operation—provisional and not decisive—which then acts as a key or as an occasional cause; on condition, of course, that the intelligence has at its disposal correct and sufficient data, and that it benefits from the concurrence of a moral health founded upon the sense of the sacred, and consequently capable of a sense of proportion as well as of aesthetic intuition. For all things are connected: if intelligence has need of rigor in a direct manner, it also has need indirectly of beauty.

PART 2
DIVINE AND UNIVERSAL ORDER

The Interplay of the Hypostases

To speak of the Absolute, is to speak of the Infinite; Infinitude is an intrinsic aspect of the Absolute. It is from the "dimension" of Infinitude that the world springs forth; the world exists because the Absolute, being such, implies Infinitude.

This Absolute-Infinite is the Sovereign Good; the *Agathon* of Plato. Now the Good—according to the Augustinian formula—tends essentially to impart itself; being the Sovereign Good, the Absolute-Infinite cannot but project the world; which is to say that the Absolute, being the Sovereign Good, comprises thereby Infinitude and Radiation.

If we were to be asked what the Absolute is, we would reply first of all that it is necessary and not merely possible Reality; absolute Reality, hence infinite and perfect, precisely; and we would add—in keeping with the level of the question asked—that the Absolute is that which, in the world, is reflected as the existence of things. Without the Absolute, there is no existence; the aspect of absoluteness of a thing is what distinguishes it from nonexistence, if one may so put it. Compared to empty space, each grain of sand is a miracle.

If furthermore we were to be asked what the Infinite is, we would reply, with the quasi-empiricist logic required by the question itself, that the Infinite is that which, in the world, appears as modes of expanse or of extension, such as space, time, form or diversity, number or multiplicity, matter or substance. In other words, and to be more precise: there is a conserving mode, and this is space; a transforming mode, and this is time; a qualitative mode, and this is form, not inasmuch as it limits, but inasmuch as it implies indefinite diversity; a quantitative mode, and this is number, not inasmuch as it fixes a given quantity, but inasmuch as it too is indefinite; a substantial mode, and this is matter, it too being without limit as is shown by the star-filled sky. Each of these modes has its prolongation—or more exactly its basis—in the animic state and beyond, for these modes are the very pillars of universal existence.

Finally, if we were to be asked what Perfection or the Sovereign Good is—for to speak of God is to speak of Goodness, as is indicated for instance by the very expression of the "Good Lord"—we would say it is that which, in the world, is manifested as qualities and, more concretely, as qualitative phenomena; perfections and perfect things. We say "that which is manifested" and not "that which is": the Absolute, the Infinite, the Good are not respectively existence, the existential categories, the qualities of things, but, precisely, all of these factors manifest what the divine Hypostases—if one may say so—are in themselves and beyond the world.

Infinitude and Perfection are intrinsic dimensions of the Absolute; but they also assert themselves "in a descending direction" and in view of cosmogonic manifestation, in which case it could be said that Perfection or the Good is the "image" of the Absolute produced by Radiation, hence by virtue of the Infinite. It is here that the divine *Māyā* comes into play, Relativity *in divinis*: whereas on the one hand the Absolute possesses Infinitude and Perfection by definition, on the other hand—in virtue of the Relativity necessarily implied by the Infinite—the Absolute gives rise to an operative Infinitude and to a manifested Good; thus to a hypostatic hierarchy "in a descending direction" and which, in the final analysis, is "creative".

The Absolute is infinite; therefore It radiates, and in radiating It projects itself; the content of this projection being the Good. The Absolute could neither radiate nor produce thereby the image of the Good if It were not itself, in its Immutability, both the Good and the Radiation, or in other words, if It did not possess these intrinsic dimensions, but which are indistinct since Relativity is transcended. This is the very foundation of what Christian doctrine terms the Hypostases.

To speak of projection is to speak of polarization: the Infinite—at the degree of *Māyā* or, more precisely, at the summit of Relativity—projects the Absolute and thus produces the image, and from the moment there is image—this is the Logos—there is polarization, that is to say refraction of the Light which in itself is indivisible. The Good refracted, or the Logos, contains all possible Perfections, It translates the Potentiality of the Essence into an inexhaustible unfolding of possibilities, and It is thus the divine "locus" of the archetypes.

Geometrically speaking, we could say that the point by its very nature contains both the circle and the rays; that being the case, it projects them. The point here stands for the Absolute; the cluster of rays, for operative Infinity; the circle, for the Projected Good, hence for the totality of perfections. This is to say that the divine Order comprises on the one hand "degrees" and on the other hand "modes": degrees in projecting itself, and modes in polarizing itself.

God is also Perfection, we have said; however, evil cannot not exist, but its existence is always limited with respect to spatial as well as to temporal extension, whereas the Sovereign Good has no limit. And yet, man as such cannot fully understand the existence of evil; there always remains a point at which man, instead of understanding concretely, has to resign himself to accepting what his sensibility and his imagination, and even his logic, do not seem able to grasp. And this is not unrelated to the fact that man as such cannot comprehend the divine nature exhaustively, even though the Intellect in principle comprehends all, for it is God who comprehends Himself in it; but this ultimate comprehension, to which man has access in principle, coincides with the Inexpressible; whereas language is man, and infinite knowledge cannot pertain to that which in human nature is part of language, thought, and desire. In other words: there is always in evil an element of unintelligibility or of absurdity, which is reducible intellectually, but not imaginatively or sentimentally, and therefore humanly; this is not a reproach, but the taking note of a natural fact. The logic of the metaphysician can be satisfied without difficulty; but human sentiment, we repeat, has no choice other than to submit, which, precisely, amounts to saying that human nature has its limits. Humanly, no one escapes the obligation to "believe in order to be able to understand" (*credo ut intelligam*).

But if evil in its concrete form is partially incomprehensible to man, the good which is abstract in practice—namely, spiritual good—is as much so; man may very well know that prayer places him before God and in contact with Mercy, but if he were capable of understanding this totally and concretely, he would spare himself many worries and anxieties; and he would better grasp, eschatologically speaking, that evil can only barely touch the free, responsible, and immortal man who gives himself to God, but not overcome him.

Let us however return to the question of privative possibility in itself: all things considered, one need not seek far for the causes of human perplexity in the face of concrete evil; if a particular phenomenon of evil seems incomprehensible to us, it is not so much because our understanding is limited as it is for the simple reason that there is nothing to understand, except in an abstract manner. This is to say that we understand perfectly that evil is either a privation or an excess and that it is necessary for such and such metaphysical reasons; we understand evil in itself, but we do not understand such and such an evil. The concrete understanding of the absurd is a contradiction in terms, the absurd being precisely that which offers nothing to our understanding, except its mere possibility and its evident falseness. If our ultimate refuge is God, intellectually as well as morally, it is because He alone is absolutely intelligible, whether we understand this *a priori* or not; He alone being that which is, and total intelligibility coinciding with pure Being.

In Trinitarian theology, the Absolute in itself corresponds to Being and Power;[1] the Infinite, to Will or Love, therefore to the function of projection or radiation; and the Good, to Intelligence or Knowledge, therefore to the polarization of the potentialities of the Essence.

The Absolute, the Good, the Infinite: *Sat, Chit, Ānanda*. In considering this analogy between the Trinity just mentioned and the Vedantic Ternary—"Being, Consciousness, Beatitude"—it could be asked what relationship there is between the Good and Consciousness (*Chit*); now the Good, from the moment that it springs as such from the Absolute—which contains it in an undifferentiated or indeterminate manner—coincides with the distinctive Consciousness which the Absolute has of itself; the divine Word, which is the "Knowledge" that God has of Himself, cannot but be the Good, God being able to know Himself as Good only.

The principle of radiation or projection—inherent in the Absolute, in the "Father"—corresponds to the "Holy Spirit", and the principle of polarization or refraction, to the "Son".[2] The "Son" is to the

---

[1] This is reflected, in the physical world, in the relationship "mass-energy". As for the notion of "Being", it should not be interpreted here in its narrowly ontological and determinative sense, but simply as a synonym for Reality.

[2] This complementarity is equally represented by "Mary" and "Jesus", whence the femininization—as regards Mary—of the *Pneuma* on the part of certain gnostics.

"Father" what the circle is to the center; and the "Holy Spirit" is to the "Father" what the radius is to the center. And as the radius, which "emanates" from the center, does not stop at the circle but traverses it, it could be said that starting from the circle, the radius is "delegated" by the circle, just as the "Spirit" emanates from the "Father" and is delegated by the "Son"; the nature of the *filioque*, at once justifiable and problematical, becomes clear with the aid of this image.

To say that the "Father" is nothing without the "Son"—we have encountered this ill-sounding expression somewhere—can mean only this, if one wishes to find a plausible meaning in it: that the Absolute would not be the Absolute without its potentiality, both hypostatic and cosmogonic, of "exteriorization", therefore also of "repetition". Between the Absolute and its projection, both intrinsic and extrinsic[3]—depending on the ontological degree—there is at once inequality and equality, which Catholic theology expresses by the elliptical notion of "subsistent relations"; "relation" refers logically to inequality, and "subsistent", to equality, which, for the theologians, abolishes in practice its contrary.[4] It can be seen from this that dogmatist thought is so to speak static and exclusive, and that it takes no account of the play of *Māyā*; in other words, it admits of no movement, no diversity of points of view and of aspects, and no degrees in Reality. It offers keys, but also veils; appeasing and protective veils assuredly, but veils which it itself will not lift.

The "Father" is always "greater" than the "Son" and the "Holy Spirit": greater than the Son, because, precisely, He is the Father—otherwise the words would be meaningless—and greater than the Holy Spirit since it emanates from the Father and not conversely.

---

[3] The expression "intrinsic projection" seems contradictory, but it comprises—like the expression "relatively absolute"—a metaphysical nuance which it is impossible to express otherwise and which, in spite of the paradox, is perfectly graspable.

[4] "The Father is greater than I" (John 14:28), but "I and the Father are one" (John 10:30). Theology does not draw all of the conclusions implied by the former; and it draws too many from the latter.

The Son is therefore always "lesser" than the Father—apart from the relationship of equality which is that of the Essence and which does not apply here—whereas in regard to the Holy Spirit, He is either greater or lesser: He is greater inasmuch as He "delegates" or "sends" the Spirit, and lesser inasmuch as He is "manifested" by it, at the time of the Incarnation and also as "Child" of the Virgin; she is the personification of the Holy Spirit, as the expressions *gratia plena* and *Mater Dei* clearly indicate.

The Holy Spirit is always lesser than the Father, in the sense that It is the Radiation of the Father, whereas It is either greater or lesser than the Son: It is greater inasmuch as It serves as the vehicle for the Son or projects Him, but lesser inasmuch as It is delegated or sent by the Son. It is thus that the radii which emanate from a point are "greater" than the circle which they project as it were, but this circle is "greater" than the radii, once it is situated at the interior of the radiation and thereby in practice assumes the central situation of the point.

The Hypostases are not "relative", that is to say "non-absolute" or "less absolute", inasmuch as they are "contained" in the Essence—this latter, according to a certain early perspective, coinciding with the "Father"—they are relative inasmuch as they "emanate" from It; if they were not "contained", they could not "emanate". The Hypostases are relative with respect to the Essence, and absolute with respect to the world, which amounts to saying—paradoxically, but necessarily—that they are "relatively absolute"; that they are so at the ontological level of "emanation", and not in essentiality where they coincide with the Absolute pure and simple.

We are here at the limit of what can be expressed; it is no one's fault if within every enunciation of this kind there remain unanswerable questions, at least with respect to a given need for logical explanation and on the plane of dialectics; for the science of the heart is beyond discussion. In any case, it is all too evident that wisdom cannot start with the intention of expressing the ineffable; rather it intends to furnish points of reference that permit us to open ourselves to the ineffable to the extent possible, and according to what is foreseen by the Will of God.

— ⫶ —

For the Christians, to say that God is one means nothing if we do not add that God is three; for the Muslims, to say that He is three amounts to denying that He is one. For the Christians, Unity underlies, so to speak, the Trinity, or at least it is not enunciated except along with the latter; for the Muslims, the Trinity—or Duality, or Quaternity—is comprised in Unity but does not enter into its definition. God being one, He is thereby—implicitly and relatively—two or three as well as a thousand.

Leaving aside the issue of denominational over-accentuation, we will say that both conceptions—the unitary and the trinitary—meet and are resolved in their archetype, which is none other than the Absolute at once immutable and radiating; being what It is, the Absolute cannot not be immutable, and It cannot not radiate. Immutability, or remaining true to Itself; and Radiation, or gift of Itself; therein lies the essence of all that is.

The Problem of Possibility

The notion of possibility gives rise *a priori* to two interpretations, the first "horizontal" and the second "vertical", analogically speaking: on the one hand we say "that is possible, therefore it can be done"; on the other hand we say, "that has been done, or that exists, therefore it was possible". In the first case, the possible is what may either be or not be, and is thus opposed to the necessary, which must be; in the second case, the possible is what can and must be, and is therefore causal and produces something which is necessary since it exists. In the latter sense, the notion of the possible corresponds to a retrospective observation, possibility being then an underlying potency[1] which is directed at a necessity of manifestation; in the other sense, the notion is prospective and opens out onto the uncertain. On the one hand, it is possible to pick fruit, therefore I can do so in principle, but it may be that I cannot do so in fact; on the other hand, I have picked fruit, therefore it was possible for me; or again, a particular fruit exists, therefore it corresponds to a possibility within earthly existence.

Starting from the more or less empirical distinction between the "possible" and the "real", one may say, in this respect, that what manifests itself is "real" and that what can either manifest itself or not is merely "possible"; but in another respect, which abolishes this distinction, it is the possible which is the real, manifestation being accidental or illusory; in this case, the possible is identified with a Platonic archetype, therefore with a concrete element in the divine Order and not with a human uncertainty. In other words, instead of limiting ourselves to distinguishing between the "possible" and the "real", which without being false is nonetheless insufficient, we ought, on the one hand, to distinguish between the contingently possible and the necessary and, on the other hand, between the principially possible and the actual; the necessary is more than the possible if this last term is taken to mean the indefinite expanse of modal and temporal contingencies, but the possible as principial potency is eminently more real than the

---

[1] "Potency" comes from the Latin *posse*, "to be able", from which, precisely, comes *possibilis*: to be potent is to be greatly "able", and thus to be rich in "possibilities". "Potentiality" is of the same order.

actual or the manifested. It goes without saying that cosmic, therefore manifested and non-principial, necessities are by definition contingent to some degree, and conversely that realized contingencies are relatively necessary.

The criterion of what the word "possible" legitimately means, is what it means in an immediate manner: that is possible which can either be or not be, a journey for example, or whatever proves its possibility by its existence, an animal species for example. Strictly speaking, it would be possible for things not to be, since necessary being belongs to the divine Principle alone; yet things are because Existence is relatively necessary by virtue of the radiating potency of Being, and because contingency, hence diversity, is necessary in its turn by virtue of the principle of particularization proper to Existence. God is both absolute Necessity and infinite Possibility; in the first respect, He transcends everything that is merely possible, whereas, in the second respect, He is, not a given possibility of course since He is absolutely necessary, but Possibility as such; this is to say, He is the Source of all that can be, or must needs be from relative necessity, therefore from participation in absolute Necessity. Possibility is potency at its root, and indetermination in its ever more far-reaching effects; God is the "All-Powerful".[2]

—— ·|· ——

What, among all the innumerable possibilities of a world, are the ones that will actually be manifested? They are those which by their nature are most in conformity, or alone are in conformity, with the realization of a determined divine plan. If we are able to visit a particular country but nonetheless will never do so, it is because if we did, we would be giving the divine plan a shift—even if trifling—that the plan does not provide for; we would be upsetting an equilibrium, although this is an absurd hypothesis, since it is impossible for any single will to pit itself against the divine Will; everything that occurs is willed by God—in a certain dimension of the divine Will—and if a particular thing does not occur, it is precisely because it does not fit into the realization of what is possible in a given case.

[2] "With men this is impossible; but with God all things are possible" (Matt. 19:26).

In the elaboration of a cosmos, as of a virgin forest, there is an immanent discriminating will that, in the jungle, will be the law of the strongest, and in the cosmos, the divine preference; it is the latter which gives things their manifestability and their existential impulse. If, in the forest, or in any biological world, the weak had the upper hand, the forest would change in aspect, thus becoming something other than what the Creator had foreseen; now the strength of particular plants is the result of a heavenly choice; to affirm the contrary would amount to maintaining that things occur that God did not wish, and that it is by chance that a forest of pines is not a field of nettles. But in all this, there are different levels of will, on God's part, that interweave, and apparently contradict one another;[3] a world is not a plain and inert block, but an infinitely variegated play of antinomies and combinations; it proceeds, however, from of a particular divine Idea, whence its homogeneous character. One particular world is not another particular world; each is what it must be.

From the point of view of the divine Subjectivity, the Will that wills evil is not the same one that wills good; from the point of view of the cosmic object, God does not will evil as such, He wills it only inasmuch as it is a constitutive element of a good, therefore inasmuch as it is a good. From another point of view, evil is never evil in its existential substance, which by definition is willed by God; evil is only evil by the cosmic accident of a privation of a good, a privation willed by God as an indirect element of a greater good. If we are reproached for introducing a duality into God, we admit this without hesitation—but not as a reproach—just as we admit all the differentiations in the Divinity, whether of hypostatic degrees, or of qualities or of energies; the very existence of polytheism, apart from the question of its possible deviations and paganization,[4] validates our premise. It is important in any case to distinguish between the divine Will with respect to existence, and the divine Will with respect to man, who is intelligence and will: in the former relationship all that exists or comes

[3] This is expressed by the ambiguity of the semi-divine demiurge in most mythologies; polytheism too is explicable by the desire—metaphorically speaking—of avoiding the pitfall of a contradictory God.

[4] Original polytheism envisages Divinity both inasmuch as it is *Ātmā* as well as with respect to *Māyā*; it is pagan only from the moment it forgets *Ātmā* and lends absoluteness to diversity, and therefore to relativity.

about is willed by God; in the latter relationship, only the truth and the good are divinely willed.

In other words, what must never be lost sight of, even indirectly, is that Omnipotence cannot encompass what is contrary to the divine Nature, namely that which is the absurd. Consequently, Omnipotence excludes the possibility that God could be other than what He is, or that He may not be able to create at all—even though He may not be able to create a given world or a given thing. Or again, while Omnipotence implies being able to abolish a particular evil, it does not imply that God could abolish evil as such, for evil, precisely, results from creation as such, hence from the radiation demanded by the nature of the Sovereign Good.

What we have just set forth brings to mind the essential distinction between God as Essence or Beyond-Being, and God as Creator or Being:[5] Beyond-Being is absolute Necessity in itself, whereas Being is absolute Necessity with respect to the world, but not with respect to Beyond-Being. Beyond-Being, or the Self, possesses the possible as an internal dimension and in virtue of its infinitude; at this level, the possible is precisely Being, or Relativity, *Māyā*. We would say consequently that Being is Possibility purely and simply; possibility necessary in itself, but contingent in its increasingly relative contents; and by definition non-absolute, in the paradoxical sense of a "lesser absoluteness" (*apara-Brahma*).[6]

As we pointed out earlier, the distinction between Possibility and possibilities is fundamental: Being is Possibility, but the Qualities of Being—which are undifferentiated in Beyond-Being and each of which coincides with the Essence—already belong to the order of possibilities; in relation to the Essence, or as the elements of a refraction or

---

[5] The term "Being" does not necessarily have this restrictive meaning since it can embrace both aspects in question and change its meaning or scope depending on the accompanying adjective or the context. Moreover, the terms *esse* and *posse*, juxtaposed and in correlation, clearly express the relation between "Beyond-Being"—or "Non-Being"—and "Being".

[6] Literally: the "non-supreme".

differentiation, these Qualities may "not be", although in themselves and with respect to their contents they share in the absolute necessity of the Essence. It follows from this that, within the order of possibilities, a distinction must be made between possible phenomena that reflect the necessity of the Principle, and others which manifest contingency as such; the former engender things, which must be; the latter engender modes, which may or may not be.

There are two notions which still need to be considered, namely that of negative or privative possibility and that of impossibility.

The manifestation of possible phenomena implies a negative contrast to the extent that this manifestation is of a contingent order: whereas Being, Possibility as such, has no opposite—nothingness being nothing and being unable therefore to be the object of any kind of experience—the most contingent manifestations of Being, earthly things for example, call forth a contrast, namely their absence, and this can be the object of some kind of experience or other. A sound, a word, a noise can be heard, but silence can likewise be experienced, so that it too is a possibility; but this is a privative possibility, symbolizing therefore in its fashion a nothingness which in fact is impossible, or precisely possible only in the purely symbolic mode under consideration here. Nevertheless, privative possibility manifests not only a particular privation or a particular absence, but also the supra-sensory or formless archetype of the phenomenon which is absent, namely, the principle which, although embracing all of its possible manifestations while being identified with none of them, maintains a silence of depth, totality, and infinitude; thus privative possibility is at the same time a possibility with a transcendent reference.

On the subject of the privative possibility that is emptiness, we would like to make the following points: it is true, and even evident, that emptiness cannot rejoin nothingness, any more than can any other privative possibility; the omnipresence of ether, and thus a subtle mode of plenitude, shows this in its own way. However, this plenitude nonetheless does represent, empirically, perfect emptiness, therefore an experience—obviously relative—of nothingness; hence, the presence of ether does not justify denying the phenomenon of spa-

tial emptiness; what cannot be produced, however, is absolute Emptiness, which would be either nothingness pure and simple—which is
possible only as a concept and as a tendency—or the Absolute as such,
therefore non-manifestable Reality. This last term must not, however,
be allowed to obscure the fact that even supreme Beyond-Being manifests itself indirectly, since no one can deny that empirical emptiness
is a kind of trace of the principial and metacosmic Void, albeit strictly
non-manifestable in itself; if we are able, provisionally and with all
due precautions, to assign a word to a reality, it is because the reality
in question is not totally unknowable to us; strictly speaking, all that
is real is, in principle, knowable.[7]

One has to be careful—be it said in passing—not to involve a
metaphysical impossibility and an indisputable physical experience in
one and the same negation: that space is not emptiness in an absolute
sense, namely the discontinuance and the very end of spatial extension, does not prevent it from being the void symbolically and empirically, as we have just noted. An analogous reservation can be made as
regards causality, for here again one has to be careful not to attribute
an absolute significance to modes of speech referring to the relative:
that like causes always produce like effects does not mean that modalities—which do not enter into causality—should always be alike,
for this precisely is what is impossible, but rather that the essential
relationship—the only one that causality envisages—is the same in all
similar instances. Analogously, to say that history repeats itself means,
not that the same effects are always produced in the same fashion, but
that in history too like causes engender like effects, the word "like"
alluding only to what applies to the causal chain, and not to what has
no relation to it. If there are days and nights, it is because the earth
turns, and not because it turns one way today and will turn another
way tomorrow owing to changes in its position; the cause is clearly in
the turning and not in "how" it turns; the imperceptible deviations do
not in any way affect the unvarying fact of rotary motion.

---

[7] To say that God is "unknowable" is, on the one hand simply a manner of speaking
which intends to emphasize that reason is limited in principle, and on the other hand
that the intellect, accidentally obscured, is limited in fact. To possess total Knowledge
is to be possessed by it: it is to be a "knower by God" (*'ārif bi 'Llāh*), in the sense that
God reveals Himself to the extent that He is, in us, both the Subject and the Object
of Knowledge.

But let us return to supreme Beyond-Being:[8] in order to distinguish it from Being,[9] it could be said that the first is "absolutely infinite" whereas the second is relatively so, which, while being tautological and even contradictory, is nevertheless a useful formulation in a language that cannot avoid ellipses; the gap between logic and transcendent truths permits these truths to occasionally transgress logic, although the converse is clearly excluded. If we leave Beyond-Being out of the equation, we are entitled then to attribute infinitude to Being; but if it is Beyond-Being that is being considered, then we shall say that the Infinite is Beyond-Being, and therefore that Being realizes this infinitude in a relative mode, thus opening the door to the outpouring of endlessly varied and hence inexhaustible possibilities.

Nothingness is, on the one hand, an intellectual notion and, on the other hand, a cosmic tendency; the notion of nothingness is identical with that of impossibility; nothingness, in other words, is total impossibility, whereas there are relative impossibilities, namely those representing situations that in principle are modifiable.

Impossibility presents itself to our mind under two aspects: impossibility in itself or nothingness, and impossibility appearing as the result of an absurd thought. For example, it is absurd to admit that a thing presents simultaneously and in the same respect mutually exclusive characteristics; but since impossibility cannot be absolute to the extent it enters into the existential categories, there are then always possibilities that tend to resolve contradictions. Thus one may say that gray has the function, "inasmuch as possible", of invalidating the impossibility of white being black; and there exists an infinity of intermediate possibilities, some bordering on the absurd, which cannot be explained otherwise, both on the plane of events as well as of forms. The impossible and nothingness do not exist, but the infinitude of Possibility lends them an at least apparent and illusory

[8] Or "Non-Being"; the *Wu-Yu* of Lao Tzu.

[9] The notion of *Esse* in Saint Thomas includes this Beyond-Being, in the same way that the Name *Allāh* refers to the two "divine Dimensions", the "Attributes" and the "Essence".

existence, and it is this principle which, in *Māyā*, draws things away from the Principle and spreads out the world in a veil of countless limitations and in the direction of a nothingness that quite obviously is never reached. But the Real is one, and this results in every limitation being at the same time, in one respect or another, a mirror of the one and only Possible and the one and only Essence.

We noted above that on God's part there are different levels of will that contradict one another in appearance. The Asharites cannot go beyond this appearance: for them the divine Will is the wish of an individual who contradicts himself because he "does what he wills"; this amounts to saying that God has the right to contradict Himself because no one has the power to prevent Him from doing so. This is the incomprehension alluded to by Ibn Arabi when he says in his *Fusūs al-Hikam* (chapter on Seth): "Certain theorists, intellectually weak, starting from the axiom that God does what He wills, have declared it lawful to maintain that God acts contrary to principles and contrary to what Reality is in itself, and therefore they have gone so far as to deny possibility (*imkān*) and allow only necessity (*wujūb*), be it absolute ("by essence") or relative ("by another"). . . . And in virtue of what is Possibility (= *Māyā*) different from Necessity (= *Ātmā*), since Necessity requires difference?[10] No one knows this difference save the Knowers in *Allāh*."

And likewise: referring to the Koranic expression "Had He willed, He would have guided all men", Ibn Arabi notes that the divine non-willing results, not from an arbitrary decision on God's part, but from the nature of particular human possibilities, this nature preceding as it were the existentiation God lends the possibilities; and Ibn Arabi concludes from this that man alone judges himself, for the final judgment is none other than an aspect of the possibility represented by a particular man. By definition, a possibility wants to be what it is, its nature is its will to be; God creates only by "giving

---

[10] This is no doubt a way of saying that the absolutely Necessary comprises Infinity which, in its turn, comprises Possibility, which by definition engenders things possible. Absolute Necessity requires Relativity, hence differentiation.

existence" to that which wants to be this or that. Possibilities are differentiated revelations of Being; they proceed from It and not from an arbitrary Will which would conceive them *ex nihilo*; and it is this diversifying and contrasting refraction that gives rise to the inverted and privative modalities of possibilities which are necessarily positive at their outset, or positive in their roots. This opposing and inverting differentiation is due to the dark pole of Relativity, of *Māyā*; this is the metaphysical basis of the "fall of the angels". *Māyā* brings forth the world by "radiation of love" and by virtue of divine Infinitude but also—through its other dimension—by centrifugal passion both dispersive and compressive; thus there is at the root of the world the luminous Logos on the one hand, and the tenebrous demiurge on the other hand; and the ultimate Cause of this second pole is, we repeat, that the Infinite cannot exclude what appears to be opposed to it, but which in reality contributes to its radiation.

In order to define more precisely the twofold meaning of the idea of the possible, we would say that a distinction should be made between an abstract possibility and a concrete possibility. An abstract possibility is what, from our human viewpoint, could either be or not be; a concrete possibility is what, for God and therefore in fact, must be. According to Ibn Arabi—still in the *Fusūs*—"a possibility is that which can either be actualized or not actualized; but, in reality, the effective solution of this alternative is implied already in what this possibility represents in its state of principial immutability". One will say that, in principle, such and such a man can take such and such a journey, but that in fact he has no reason for undertaking it or lacks the means to do so; this journey is therefore an impossibility *de facto*; more profoundly, it is also an impossibility pure and simple, given the nature and the destiny of this man. Thus what is possible in principle is here no more than a rational conjecture or an assessment of probabilities; it amounts to saying: if this man were not himself, if he were someone else, his destiny would allow him to take such a journey; and so on and so forth.

As for the distinction between a theoretical possibility and a practical one, it is entirely contingent: a possibility is practical—whether actual or not—when it enters into the normal conditions of a thing; a possibility is theoretical when it requires abnormal conditions, hence hard to realize or even unrealizable according to common experience.

But in what does the characteristic nature of possibility reside if everything is predetermined, with things being unable to be other than they are? Being—Possibility—is made of Freedom and Necessity; it is free because it is infinite, and necessary because it is absolute, a polarity which translates in its way the undifferentiated nature of Beyond-Being. Now the two poles are always present in all things, but with either the one or the other predominating; in things that are merely possible, it is the aspect of freedom that veils the aspect of necessity, whereas in things that are actual, it is the aspect of necessity which predominates, at least with respect to their actuality, but not necessarily to their content which may be a manifestation of freedom; a bird's flight is free, but it is predestined, hence necessary, since it is actual and not merely principial. It may be difficult for human reason to reconcile these two poles, and it is very tempting to deny them; the difficulty is not, however, greater than in the case of the boundlessness of space or time, which we are obliged to accept even if it is impossible for us to imagine it.

"With God, all things are possible": this phrase from the Gospels refers to the eruption, into the domain of earthly existence, of the divine Omnipotence in view of a miracle whether physical or spiritual. Only the eruption of Being into a particular segment of existence, namely the human microcosm, can explain man's crossing beyond the servitudes of the "cosmic wheel" into the state of divine Permanence.

Possibilities are the veils that on the one hand restrict and on the other hand manifest the absolutely Real. Possibility as such, in the singular and in an absolute sense, is the supreme Veil, the one which envelops the mystery of Unicity and at the same time unfolds it, while remaining immutable and deprived of nothing; Possibility is none other than the Infinitude of the Real. To speak of Infinitude is to speak of Potentiality; and to affirm that Possibility as such, or Potentiality, both veils and unveils the Absolute is merely a way of expressing the duodimensionality—in itself undifferentiated—which we can analytically discern in the absolutely Real. Similarly, we can discern in it a tri-dimensionality—it too intrinsically undifferentiated, yet the harbinger of a possible unfolding: these dimensions are "Being", "Consciousness", and "Bliss". It is in virtue of the third element—immutable in itself—that divine Possibility overflows and gives rise, "through love", to this mystery of exteriorization that is the universal Veil, whose warp is made of the worlds and whose weft is made of beings.

Structure and Universality of the
Conditions of Existence

The sensible phenomena which surround us, and of which we are physically a part, are manifested through matter, form, and number; they are situated in what presents itself to us as space and time. The fundamental matter is ether, from which spring the four sensible elements; the fundamental or initial form is the sphere; and the initial number is unity. Matter is the sensible manifestation of existence itself; form is the manifestation of an "idea", hence of a particular possibility or of an archetype, and in the final analysis of an aspect of divine nature, insofar as the form is positive and essential, not privative and accidental; lastly, number manifests the limitlessness of cosmic possibility, and, in the final analysis, the infinitude of the Possible as such. The immediate point of departure of the sensible world was a unique sphere made of ether, or a "cloud", as diverse traditions express it;[1] this image applies moreover to the particular "creation" of the human species and all animal and vegetable species. If ether represents pure existence, the sphere is the image of the archetype as such, and unity in its turn reflects the Principle laden with its innumerable potentialities.

Matter extends—starting from its base, ether—from extreme subtlety to extreme solidity; one could also say: from substantiality to accidentality. Form evolves—starting from the sphere—between perfect simplicity and indefinite complexity; and number goes from unity to totality. Space goes from the ungraspable point to limitless extension; and time, from the instant to perpetuity. Each of these starting points, with its indefinite unfolding, offers an image of the supreme Principle realizing its potentialities in that mysterious direction which is relativity or contingency; but at the same time, this unfolding itself testifies in its own way to the intrinsic Infinitude and to the hypostatic modes of God.

---

[1] This ethereal "cloud" marking the eruption of a subtle energy into the sensory domain.

—— ⋰ ——

Existence is perceived by a subject, and what it perceives is contents in containers, namely matter-energy, forms, and numbers, all situated in space and time. The first of these containers, space, is static and conserving; the second container, time, is dynamic and transforming. In the order of contents, matter is static, but its complement, energy, is dynamic;[2] form is static by its determining outlines, but number is dynamic by its augmenting and diminishing function.

The bipolarity object-subject signifies that each one of the existential conditions comprises an objective aspect and a subjective aspect; but there are also the two poles principle and manifestation, by virtue of which each existential condition has an aspect that is principial or abstract, and another that is manifested or concrete.

In fact, objective space and time coincide respectively with abstract space and time, while the subjective aspects of the two conditions coincide with their concrete aspects; and the same holds true for the other existential conditions. The difference between what we here term "abstract" and "objective" is simply that the first of these terms designates the condition of existence in itself, whereas the second relates to the structure of that condition, to the dimensions of space, for example; and as for the terms "concrete" and "subjective", the first designates the condition inasmuch as it is "illustrated" by particular contents, whereas the second takes into account the position of the subject as well, which amounts finally to the distinction between general or collective experience and particular or individual experience. To be precise: we term here "abstract" that which, escaping our direct experience, remains in fact more or less notional; no one can experience pure space, thus it will be in practice abstract with respect

---

[2] One can distinguish either five or six conditions of sensorial existence, according to whether matter is dissociated or not from energy; a seventh condition could even be added, namely subjectivity inasmuch as it is sensory and rational consciousness. It is perhaps worth recalling here the Peripatetic "categories": substance or the thing (*substantia*), quantity, quality, relation, doing (*actio*), undergoing (*passio*), place (*ubi*), moment (*quando*), situation (*situs*), having (*habitus*). But these categories are subjective and mental in the sense that they apply far more to notional genres than to the objective principles or phenomena that determine them; moreover, this enumeration is neither rigorous nor exhaustive, its value rather being indicative.

to the contents which measure it, either in a static or dynamic manner.[3] By contrast, something is objective which, whether abstract or concrete, is situated on the outside of our observing consciousness; in other words, a thing is objective inasmuch as it exists independently of our individual or collective consciousness, while being subjective inasmuch as it is a possible content of that consciousness.

Moreover, even the abstract in the proper and strict sense of the word is not devoid of concrete reality which it transcribes in the form of a notion—unless it is only a matter of purely contingent and artificial ideas—for the fact that liberty, for example, is mentally an abstraction in no way prevents it from deriving all of its reality, hence its efficaciousness, from principial Infinitude—which coincides with All-Possibility—and this through diverse hypostatic and cosmic degrees;[4] the same is true for the correlative idea of necessity, the necessary referring in the final analysis to the Absolute, hence to the pure Real.

— ·∴· —

Concrete space is the amplitude, the outlining, and the location of spatial phenomena; abstract space is extension in itself, which phenomena render measurable.

Objective space has three dimensions: height, breadth, and length or depth;[5] in subjective space, by contrast, there is a center and a periphery—the subject itself and the outer limits of its experience—and one distinguishes between what is above and below, in front and behind, to the right and to the left.

Similarly for time, *mutatis mutandis*: it is either abstract or concrete, either objective or subjective. Concrete time is the changing of phenomena; abstract time is the duration which this change renders measurable.

---

[3] Like the containers space and time, the container subject is relatively abstract and fully concrete at the same time: concretely, it is a fabric made of memories and tendencies, of destiny and character, whereas abstractly it is reduced to the consciousness of the "I".

[4] One will here recall the medieval controversies between Nominalists and Realists.

[5] Let us note that the word "depth" applies conventionally either to the dimension of height or length, according to the imaginative accentuation.

Objective time is so to speak a spiroidal movement comprising four phases, and this movement is qualitatively ascending or descending, according to what the period of the full cycle requires; this is to say that time is like a wheel which turns, this rotation being itself subordinated to a greater rotation, exactly as the rotation of the earth is inscribed within the circumambulation of the planet around the sun.[6] As for subjective time, the definition of which is just as basic as that of the corresponding space, it is divided into present, past, and future: what we are, what we were, and what we will be, and in addition what our surroundings are, were, and will be.

The idea of an absolutely empty time is just as contradictory as the idea of an absolutely empty space. If one removed from space all of its contents, there would remain nothing more than the mere possibility of phenomenal existence: the possibility of simultaneous phenomena conjoined to the possibility—temporal, precisely—of successive phenomena. The possibility of space and time comes with that of things.

To return to subjective space and time, there is not only general subjectivity concerning the subject as such, there is also particular subjectivity which concerns such and such a subject: that is to say there is a dilation, or on the contrary a contraction, of space or of time according to the disposition of a particular human or animal subjectivity; both the dilation and the contraction can be either qualitative or privative. It is said that in the golden age time was longer than in later epochs; conversely, pleasure or happiness seem to shorten outward time, whereas the contrary experience prolongs it. In ecstasy, or even simply in states of contemplation, a moment can have the subjective value of an hour or a day, and conversely; but in this last case—when a long duration appears short—there is no contraction, there is participation, in itself dilating, in eternity, therefore entry into the "eternal present". Similar remarks could be made about space: for the child, a small garden appears to be a whole world; for certain adults, the whole world appears to be too narrow;[7] with the spiritual man the one does

---

[6] We refer here, without entering into details, to the Hindu doctrine of cosmic cycles; a doctrine which moreover is diverse, but nonetheless homogeneous with regard to the essential.

[7] In addition, objective space itself presents certain fundamental aspects of subjectivity—this has been observed in the astronomical order—but practically speaking this remains outside our topic since it in no way affects the characteristic structure of

not exclude the other, for this lower world is an exile while being at the same time a reflection of Paradise. The sage combines hope with gratitude, or old age with childhood.

If the "dilation" of duration—the "slowness" of time—manifests *a priori* a positive reality, the present is also positive inasmuch as it manifests celestial intemporality or the "eternal beatitude"; similarly, if spatial limitlessness has about it something beatific, there is also the complementary symbolism of the center, which strictly speaking takes us out of space while offering us a kind of celestial security.

In space, the objective dimension of height gives rise to the subjective opposition between high and low: high signifying the element "heaven", and low, the element "earth", possibly "hell", but also, very positively, the element "depth" and thus "heart" and "immanence";[8] this depth refers to the unitive virtuality of the Intellect and consequently, in the final analysis, to the divine "Self". In an analogous manner, the objective dimension of width gives rise to the subjective opposition—that is to say, dependent upon the empirically central situation of a subject—between right and left, which refers either to the complementarity between activity and passivity, or to the moral alternative between a good and an evil. Similarly again, the objective dimension of length or depth gives rise to the subjective opposition— that is to say determined by the position of the subject—between what is in front and what is behind; that is to say, between what has been passed—or left behind in whatever way—and what is unknown and offers itself to our experience.

Objective time, we said, involves four phases, the most striking examples of which are the four seasons of the year; now each one of these phases can be situated in one of the three subjective dimensions of time, namely the past, the present, and the future. The respective meanings of spring, summer, autumn, and winter—or of morning,

space, and results from the evident relativity—or from the non-absoluteness—of the spatial and temporal conditions.

[8] Which evokes the positive symbolism of the cave, complementary in relation to the symbolism of the mountain; immanence and transcendence.

day, evening, night, or again of childhood, youth, maturity, and old age—these meanings are part of our common experience and thus require no commentary; however, it is worth mentioning something about the symbolism—also perfectly concrete—of the three subjective dimensions of time.

Positively, the past refers to the origin, to primordial and normative perfection, to the "lost Paradise", it evokes therefore the virtue of fidelity; negatively, it evokes immaturity now transcended, imperfection overcome, the "world" that has been given up for the sake of God. Positively, the future signifies the goal, the ideal to be realized, the Paradise to be gained, it thus evokes the virtue of hope; negatively, it is the forgetting of the origin, infidelity to the primordial norm, the loss of innocent and happy childhood. It is the positive sense that prevails here in fact, just as it is the negative sense that prevails for the past; for "he who puts his hand to the plow and looks back, is not fit for the Kingdom of God"; and "let the dead bury their dead".

As for the present, it is, negatively, forgetting the Origin as well as the Goal, hence attachment to the moment—forever fleeting—of current pleasure; but positively, the present signifies the virtue of faith, which determines both the virtue of hope and that of fidelity, the one not going without the other, just as there is no past without future, and conversely.

Just as the Infinite or All-Possibility is the complement, both intrinsic and extrinsic, consubstantial and proceeding, of the Absolute or All-Reality, so time is both inherent in space and proceeds from it; and the same is true for the relationship between matter and its dynamic potentiality: to speak of matter, or mass, or ether, is to speak of energy, possibility of action, hence of change and consequently of time.[9]

---

[9] The current idea that energy is "before" matter and engenders it under certain conditions, takes us to a great extent—and in the final analysis even completely—out of the world which is supposed to be sensible in principle. The notion then of energy takes on another meaning, for pre-material energy is of the animic order, hence properly "non-material", something that materialist science could never admit. It should be noted, however, that the borderline between the material and animic states has nothing absolute about it, at least in principle.

We have made the distinction above between an objective and a subjective space, and likewise for the temporal condition; likewise again, each of the other conditions of existence—matter along with energy, form, and number—is subjected to the bipolarity object-subject. Subjective matter is our concrete sensory experience, objective matter being what provokes it; subjective form is the aspect of form that presents itself to our senses, for no one can perceive a form from all sides at once; subjective number is that which offers itself to our experience, not that which exists in fact, bearing in mind the necessary repetition of all possible phenomena. It would be totally false to deduce from all this, as do the subjectivists, that there is no adequate knowledge, for this is to forget that adequation constitutes the sufficient reason for the intelligence and thus its very essence; even a limited knowledge is adequate to the exact degree that it is a knowledge and not something else.

Just as energy is the complement—in the sense of the term *shakti*—of mass or matter, and just as time is the complement of space, so likewise there is a relation of complementarity between form and number, in the sense that number indicates quantity, and form quality; this must not make us lose sight of the fact that number possesses a qualitative aspect—as was taught by Pythagoras and as is shown by geometrical figures, or as is proven by the very notions of numerical richness and power[10]—and, conversely, that form possesses a quantitative aspect to the extent that it lacks content and thus appears as one accident among others.

Form relates to the idea of the center; in space, form, taken in itself and in isolation, is always central. Number, for its part, refers to extension, it reveals so to speak the contingency of form; God alone is one and unique because He alone is absolute. Form is the concrete center, and likewise, the act is the concrete present; the sacred form contains all of space, there is nothing outside it, just as, for its part, the sacred act synthesizes time, its repetition being but an accident or an appearance; and the same holds true for the spatial repetition of the

---

[10] The numbers two, three, or four, for example, are quantities, but duality, trinity, and quaternity are, on the contrary, qualities. The triangle expresses a potentiality of the One and not a contingent addition; and let us specify that the trinity has in a certain way priority over the other two hypostatic numbers because, being odd, it thereby reflects unity more directly.

sacred form. What form and contemplation are for space, the event and the act are for time.

— .:. —

Matter-energy, form, number, space, and time are the conditions of existence that is more or less sensible; but this necessarily approximate definition cannot preclude that these conditions be universal in their roots, which are principles, and that their empirical manifestations be but the prolongations of these roots in our world. Indeed matter refers in the final analysis to the divine Substance; form reflects the first hypostatic auto-determination, the divine Logos; number refers to the inexhaustible divine Unity as well as to the hypostases that proceed from it; space is in its essence the expanse of the divine Manifestation, total Possibility; and time is, according to the same principial relation, the rhythm of the universal cycles, the "days and nights of Brahmā". What is characteristic for our world is not the presence of these conditions, but the particularity of their manifestation with respect to their principial roots; however these particular modes which offer themselves to our experience have quite clearly nothing arbitrary about them, precisely because they retrace ontological principles, dimensions of *Ātmā* prolonging or projecting itself by and in *Māyā*.

What holds true for the Universe applies equally to the soul, for what the macrocosm is, so is the microcosm in its turn and in its fashion. The soul is "matter" by its existential substance, "form" by its individuality, "number" by its subjectivity which can only be unique; it is "space" by its expansion, and "time" by its cycles. Or again, it is "spatial" by its memory, since space conserves, and "temporal" by its imagination, since time changes and transforms;[11] it could perhaps be added that reason refers to number, since it calculates, and intuition to form, since it perceives directly and by synthesis.

Our spiritual attitude is "concentration" with respect to spatial extension—outward or inward—and it is "perseverance" with respect to duration; for space, with its innumerable contents, tends to distract

---

[11] But one could also maintain, conversely and secondarily, that memory is temporal inasmuch as it refers to the past, and imagination is spatial inasmuch as it contains the diversity of things.

and to seduce us, whereas time, with its events, tends to dominate us and to change us; both time and space seem to want to ravish us away from ourselves. By concentration, we leave phenomena aside, and by perseverance, we fix this attitude in duration; for it is not enough to know how to concentrate perfectly, one must also think of doing it; what is the point of possessing a talisman if one forgets to make use of it.[12] To the "spatial" virtue of detachment must be joined the "temporal" virtue of vigilance.

It is thus that the fundamental conditions of existence give rise, in the human microcosm, to more than one spiritual perfection. With regard to "space", the soul makes itself empty for God; with regard to "time", it makes itself pure movement, reflux towards the Inward, leaping towards Mercy and abandon to it. With regard to "form", the soul fixes itself in contemplation of divine Beauty;[13] with regard to "number", it makes itself multiple by projecting its prayer, its sacramental act, into duration, while bringing thereby the multiple back to unity. With regard to "matter" or "substance", the soul makes itself motionless before the Immutable and is extinguished in the intellective vision of the Essence; finally, with regard to "energy", it identifies itself virtually with its own source, which is pure Life and which opens out onto the "Self" at once transcendent and immanent.

Without leaving the question of the human participation in the hypostatic dimensions and in their cosmic or terrestrial prolongations, we shall permit ourselves to insert a remark here. The arts are connected in various ways with the existential conditions: thus, the plastic arts pertain to space, whereas poetry and music pertain to time; poetry and music are auditive and "inward", whereas painting, sculpture, architecture are visual and "outward". Dance combines space and time, while summarizing the other conditions: form being represented by the body of the dancer; number, by his movements; matter, by his

[12] Thus it is not for nothing that the Sufis, in conformity moreover with Koranic language, term spiritual concentration "remembrance of God"; the man who dedicates himself to it, and who realizes it profoundly, being the "son of the Moment", which is not without relation to the symbolism of the frontal eye.

[13] "Keeping the spirit within the confines of the body", as the Hesychasts would say; now the body is our theomorphic form, it is therefore holy and sin remains external to it. Sin is man's, but the pure form is God's, for it testifies to the "idea", not to the accident.

flesh; energy, by his life; space, by the extension that contains his body; time, by the duration that contains his movements. It is thus that the Dance of Shiva summarizes the six conditions of existence, which are like the dimensions of *Māyā*, and *a priori* those of *Ātmā*; if the Dance of Shiva, the *Tāndava*, is said to bring about the destruction of the world, this is because, precisely, it brings *Māyā* back to *Ātmā*. And it is thus that all sacred dance brings the accidents back to the Substance, or the particular, accidental, and differentiated subject back to the universal, substantial, and one Subject; this is moreover the function of music and, more or less indirectly, of all inspired art; it is above all the function of love in all its forms, whence the intrinsically sacred character of love and the arts, yet ambiguous under the reign of human decadence.

The supreme Principle is pure Substance, which is to say It is without accident. Without accident, or namely: without contingency, without limit, and without imperfection; contingency being opposed to Absoluteness as the accident is opposed to the Substance; and similarly, limit being opposed to Infinitude, and imperfection to Perfection, or to the Potentiality of the Good. All of this evokes, by distant analogy, the nature of essential and non-qualified matter on the one hand, namely ether, and on the other hand that of the substantiality of the saintly soul, or of the contemplative soul in a state of *vacare Deo*, "emptiness for God".

If it is permissible to establish correspondences between the hypostatic dimensions of the Divinity and the conditions of universal, or more specifically sensorial, existence—and it is in the nature of things that these can be established, Reality being one—we would say that God's "matter" is pure Being, which contains the creative Power; this "matter" is pure Substance, pure Spirit, and man must participate therein to the extent of his possibilities and by virtue of his theomorphism. God's "form" is that He is absolutely simple, hence indivisible, or that He is absolutely perfect, hence the source of every possible perfection. His "number" is that He is one and unique, that is to say transcendent and unequalable while at the same time inexhaustible. His "space" is that He is here and that everything is in Him; and His "time" is that He is now, in a principial actuality that contains all movement, all rhythm, all cyclical unfolding.

God is the Absolute, and being the Absolute He is equally the Infinite;[14] being at once the Absolute and the Infinite, intrinsically and without duality, He is also the Perfect. Now Absoluteness is reflected in space by the point or the center; in time, by the moment or the present; in matter, by ether, which serves as the vehicle of energy; in form, by the sphere; in number, by unity.

Infinitude, for its part, determines space through extension; time, through duration; matter, through substantial indefiniteness; form, through the limitless diversity of formal possibilities; number, through quantitative limitlessness.

As for the divine Perfection—from which all manifested perfections derive—it is reflected in space by the contents of matter inasmuch as they express either simple existence, or the divine Qualities of which space serves as the vehicle. And the same for time, matter-energy, form, and number: time comprises by definition concrete phases, matter-ether gives rise to the sensible elements, form reveals Perfection through diverse modes of beauty or of functionality, number comprises the numerical principles which are so many qualities, the symbols of which are above all the figures of geometry. It is thus that the existential conditions of the Universe testify to the divine Perfection at the same time that they testify to the other hypostatic mysteries.

God's simplicity coincides with creative potentiality; likewise, the fundamental form, the sphere, represents the potentiality of all subsequent and more or less differentiated forms; and it is thus that each one of the existential conditions comprises a potentiality which corresponds to its nature.

---

[14] It is important never to lose sight of the fact that the term "God" designates the Divinity, either in all its possible aspects—hence also beyond every aspect—or in some particular aspect, notably that of the Creator. It is necessarily thus because this term cannot contain in itself a privative nuance.

Concerning form once again, let us point out that formal perfection, even if complex, always expresses simplicity, and it does so by the logic—and thereby the harmony—of its complexity, hence by its homogeneity, its univocity, and its spiritual transparency; beauty unfolds the fan of the potentialities of the Sovereign Good, which is simple but inexhaustible. In an analogous manner, qualitative number always expresses a mode of differentiation of Unity; far from contradicting Unity by quantity, it manifests it under a particular aspect of its plenitude, which is shown not only by Pythagorean numbers or geometrical figures, but also, in a more immediate fashion, by the mathematical divisions of unity.

—— ·⁝· ——

Certainly, God is ineffable, nothing can describe Him or enclose Him in words; but on the other hand, truth exists, that is to say that there are conceptual points of reference which provide a sufficient expression of the nature of God; otherwise our intelligence would not be human, which amounts to saying that it would not exist, or simply that it would be inoperative with respect to what constitutes the reason for man's existence.

God is both unknowable and knowable, a paradox which implies—on pain of absurdity—that the relationships are different, first of all on the plane of mere thought and then in virtue of everything that separates mental knowledge from that of the heart; the first is a "perceiving", and the second a "being". "The soul is all that which it knows", said Aristotle; it is necessary to add that the soul is able to know all that which it is; and that in its essence it is none other than That which is, and That which alone is.

PART 3
HUMAN WORLD

Outline of a Spiritual Anthropology

At the summit of the ontological pyramid—or rather beyond all hierarchy—we conceive of the Absolute, that by definition comprises both Infinitude and Perfection: Infinitude that radiates intrinsically and extrinsically, namely that contains the potentialities of the Absolute, on the one hand, and, on the other, projects them; and Perfection which is identified with these potentialities and that, by the effect of projection into Relativity, gives rise to all possible qualities: in the divine Being, in the world, and in ourselves. If the Absolute is pure Reality, the Infinite will be Possibility, whereas Perfection or the Good will be the totality of the contents of the Infinite.

Now the contents or modes of the divine Perfection pertain essentially to the order of Knowledge, Love, and Power, and this evokes the human faculties of intelligence, sentiment, and will. The substance of divine Perfection is the divine Subject inasmuch as It knows and loves, and that in knowing and loving, It wills; on the one hand Knowledge and Love cannot represent an irreducible duality, they cannot but be two modes of the same Subject, and on the other hand both Love and Knowledge are extended by a single "energy" which is Power or Will, precisely. For Will is not an end in itself: one cannot will except by virtue either of a knowledge or of a love.

In God, Knowledge, Love, and Power are absolute; but they are also infinite and perfect, since God is Absoluteness, Infinitude, and Perfection. Thus this ternary, which is only differentiated in the wake of its ontological projection, has to be found in the Absolute Itself and super-eminently so, hence it is found in the divine Essence, albeit in an undifferentiated manner, so that it can be affirmed that the Essence is Knowledge, or Love, or Power, but not that it contains these realities in distinctive mode as is the case on the level of the ontological-cosmological projection.

—— ·:· ——

All "anthropology" depends on a "theology" in the sense that any science of man must be an extension of a science of God, for: "Let us

65

make man in our image, after our likeness."[1] To speak of a "spiritual anthropology" is already a tautology—for by definition man entails spirit—but it is justified in a world which, having forgotten the divine, no longer knows what is human.

God is "pure Spirit": which is to say, implicitly, that He is at once Knowledge, Love, and Power. Power—or "Will"—is related either to Knowledge or to Love; each of these two "Energies" or "Hypostases" is prolonged by a Power proper to it, then by an Activity deriving from this Power.

Similarly for man: being made of spirit, he is made of knowledge and love—or of intelligence and sentiment—then of will, the latter having to be inspired by either one or the other of these two faculties. Knowledge and love proceed from the spirit as light and heat proceed from the sun; in the latter case, these two energies or functions remain in a quasi-undifferentiated state, which is to say that they are indistinguishable in practice from the very substance of the luminary.

In other words: there is in man—as in God, his Prototype—a single spirit, and this spirit is knowledge and love; and there is a will that prolongs each of these and that in turn is polarized into intention and activity, according to whether this will is intrinsic and latent, or on the contrary extrinsic and efficient.

The reality of God and that of our final ends determine at one and the same time: our conviction; our happiness; our activity; our virtue. Conviction pertains to intelligence; happiness, to sentiment; activity, to the will inasmuch as it is an extension of intelligence; virtue, to the will inasmuch as it is an extension of sentiment. Intelligence, in discerning the real, establishes conviction or certitude; sentiment, in loving the good in all its forms, enjoys happiness; and the will, in their wake, enables both spiritual activity and virtue, or contemplative concentration and moral conformity. In other words, the reality of God and of our final ends determine all that we are.

---

[1] "Image"—taken in the sense of something "relatively absolute"—denotes that man, on account of his deiformity, can in no way be a relative degree of animality; whereas "likeness", on the contrary, means that in another respect the analogy between God and man can only be relative, otherwise precisely God would not be the Absolute. We are compelled to add here that there are animal species which in their way are nobler than certain human individuals, this is all too obvious.

—— .⋮. ——

We have said that man is knowledge and love and that each of these elements is extended by the power that is adjoined to it; in other words, man is intelligence and sentiment, and each of these elements determines a third element, the will. If in this perspective intelligence-knowledge has as its complement sentiment-love, it is because this complementarity is in their nature; it is the polarity of the masculine and the feminine. According to another perspective, equally possible, what has precedence is not contrasting complementarity but, on the contrary, affinity: we would say then that man is made of intelligence and will—will being the immediate secondary mode of intelligence—and that it is sentiment or the feeling soul, in short, the affective faculty, which is an extension of both will and intelligence.

But one could equally place intelligence alone at the summit, and consider will and sentiment as its subordinate extensions, the will appearing then as masculine, and sensibility as feminine; together they constitute our character, which in fact combines what we will and what we love; this is the domain of the virtues. This way of looking at things—inasmuch as it places intelligence at the summit—pertains, as does the preceding one, to the intellective perspective; in both cases, the motive force of the path is Truth, Idea, Intellection, and not some threat or seduction.[2]

The perspective of love, on the contrary, places love at the summit and views intelligence and will solely as functions in the service of love; and love participates in the divine Love and is meant to melt in it; whence the sensualist epistemology proper to this perspective. Moreover, this perspective readily makes love coincide with will: where there is "loving", there is "willing"; in which case, intelligence or "knowing" are more or less reduced to dogmatic speculation and to apologetic activity, or even simply to a pious acknowledgment of the dogmas.

---

[2] Starting from the axiom that integral spirituality comprises by definition a doctrine and a method, we would say that doctrine is linked, to some degree or other, to discriminative and contemplative intelligence—active and passive, if one will—whereas the method comprises operative will and stimulating and interiorizing sensibility. The initiatic qualification combines all these elements.

Man, we have said, is made of intelligence, sentiment, and will; now the notion of "sentiment" is no doubt ambiguous due to the fact that there is a pejorative prejudice attached to it: one generally distinguishes between reason and sentiment, attributing to sentiment a character of unrealistic subjectivity, hence of arbitrariness and passion, whereas reason is supposedly objective; and in so doing, one loses sight of the fact, on the one hand, that reason is objective only on condition of basing itself on exact data and of proceeding correctly, and, on the other hand, that sentiment lacks objectivity only when it is excessive or misplaced, hence erroneous, not when it is justified by its object and is therefore a kind of adequation; love of holy or noble things, even to the extent that it is only sentimental, is in conformity with reality, which is not at all the case with skeptical, agnostic, or atheistic rationalism.

"God is Love": divine Love is not identical with human sentiment, but the latter is analogous to divine Love. Human sentiment reflects, in its essential function—which is the faculty of loving—a hypostatic quality, and consequently it cannot have a merely privative character and be opposed in practice to intelligence.

Intelligence, sentiment, will; or truth, virtue, freedom.

In our heart, the elements knowledge, love, and power—or intelligence, sentiment, and will—are combined as so many dimensions of one and the same deiform subjectivity. Outside our heart, these faculties become dissociated in the sense that intelligence seems to reside in the brain or the mind, and sentiment or affectivity in the soul, the *psyche*; the will, and with it the capacity to act, is then combined with each of these regions—for we have need of will in order to think the virtues as well as to practice them—but at the same time, its seat is the heart, which in this case assumes an extrinsic and particular role independently of its intrinsic character of synthesis and root. In other words: although the substantial dimensions of the heart-intellect are knowledge, love, and power—intelligence, sentiment, will—we can consider the heart as the region of the will alone if we attribute intelligence to the mind and sentiment to the soul, in which case our perspective is more exterior; and we can do so with all the more reason given that, in a certain respect, the will is identified with the subject, with the individual who "wills"; who "wills" because he "loves".

However: as the heart is in itself the seat or the organ both of sentiment and intelligence as well as of will, it must be said that a sentiment comes from the heart to the extent that it is profound, exactly as is the case with knowledge.[3] Certainly, thought pertains to the brain or to the mind, but intuitive knowledge, which is not the fruit of reasoning, pertains to the heart; similarly, ordinary sentiment, determined entirely by phenomena, comes from the soul or from the sensibility, but profound sentiment, which is nourished *ab intra* by the very essence of love—while most often having external perceptions as its occasional cause—comes from the heart and not from the animic sensibility alone; for the heart by its nature is love as well as knowledge and power. It is therefore rootedness in the heart which characterizes the greatness of this sentiment, and not the mere phenomenon of love as such; this is clearly the case with mystical love, which is inspired only secondarily or incidentally by external factors; but such is also the case with natural love to the extent that it is profound, or in other words, to the degree that its quality rejoins, in depth, love itself.

Knowledge and love come from the heart-intellect, but it is not with the heart that we are able to think and feel; by contrast, it is with the heart—with pure subjectivity—that we are able to concentrate our spirit, and that is why we say that the will in general and concentration in particular pertain to the heart, even though the heart is not limited in its depths to this function and possesses equally and *a priori* knowledge and love. The mind for its part receives its light from the heart, and its power is to comprehend, to discern, to think; and in so doing it opens the way to Intellection, which, however, it cannot produce. As for the soul, it can love the good, or things that are good; and in loving them, it must practice them, otherwise it excludes itself from the happiness conferred by good things—love comprising in itself beauty, goodness, and beatitude. In a word: if the mind permits

---

[3] Thus, common opinion is far from being mistaken when it equates the heart with love; as for the intellective character of the heart, it goes without saying that ordinary language cannot express it adequately.

comprehension, and the heart in its turn concentration, the soul has the power of being virtuous, and consequently of being happy through its very nature.

There is no valid virtue without piety, and there is no authentic piety without virtue; which means that these two coincide, and also that the emphasis is on piety inasmuch as piety relates more directly to God. Consequently, we could say that if intelligence enables discernment, and will concentration, sentiment enables piety, devotion, the sense of the sacred, and then gratitude and generosity; this attitude being linked to the qualities at once divine and cosmic of Beauty, Goodness, and Happiness.

There are two ways of viewing the modes of human subjectivity: either we consider them with respect to their functions, in which case we distinguish intelligence, sentiment, and will; or else we consider them as regions, in which case we distinguish between the world of the heart and that of the brain, the three faculties acting in both sectors or at both levels.

Normally and primordially, human intelligence realizes a perfect equilibrium between the intelligence of the brain and that of the heart: the first is the rational capacity with the various skills connected to it; the second is intellectual or spiritual intuition, or in other words it is the eschatological realism that permits one to choose the saving truth even without any mental speculation. Cardiac intelligence, even when reduced to its minimum, is always right; it is from this that faith is derived when it is profound and unshakeable, and such is the intelligence of a great number of saints. Nevertheless, the absolute norm or the ideal is the plenitude—and not the sufficient minimum—of cardiac intelligence and the perfect unfolding of dialectical intelligence.

The treasures of inner science must in fact be able to establish and transmit themselves: to establish themselves, for mental formulation contributes to the actualization and assimilation of the immanent lights of the heart, and therein lies moreover the role of meditation; to transmit themselves, for cardiac intuition must be able to radiate as do all good things. On the one hand, the essential certitudes are everything; but on the other hand, man needs to exteriorize himself the better to be able to interiorize himself; synthesis requires analysis; man, who is as if suspended between two dimensions, cannot do without language. Without the heart, there would be neither message nor doctrine; yet the well-formulated idea is necessary for the awakening of immanent knowledge. To say that mental intelligence—when it is what it ought to be—is inspired by that of the heart-intellect, is another way of saying that the intelligence of the heart manifests itself in and by that of the mind.

The mind is the moon, and the heart is the sun: even though the brightness of the moon is nothing other than light, this light belongs to the sun and to no other source. In the heart, knowledge coincides with love; the heart delegates truth to the mind, and virtue to the soul. This is to say that intelligence is pious to the extent that it is total.

The fact that spiritual realism, or faith, pertains to the intelligence of the heart and not to that of the mind, enables one to understand that in spirituality, the moral qualification takes precedence over the intellectual qualification, and by far.

The refusal to understand a transcendent truth lies moreover less in the intelligence than in the temperament, the imagination, the will; which means that the obstacle lies either simply in attachment to the world and to the ego, or on the contrary in an innocent and honorable limitation of the heart-intellect but not necessarily of the heart-love; otherwise there would be no narrow-minded saints. In any case, familiarity with transcendent concepts is far from being a guarantee of realizational capacity; thus, spiritual realization can content itself with key notions, not very demanding intellectually but nonetheless anchored in the knowledge of the heart and centered on a virtuality of Intellection.

The most extensive metaphysical knowledge is subjectively superficial and can go astray if it is purely bookish, and similarly, the most efficacious social virtues are worth nothing spiritually if they are not given value by devotion and the sense of the sacred. Since piety is "supernaturally natural" to man, a virtue without piety is tainted with pride, and for that reason loses all its value; and similarly, since Intellection also springs from our "natural supra-nature", an idea which we grasp only from without and in a mental form, is not a "knowledge" to which we can lay claim, even though we have a certain right to it according to our sincerity and also to our piety, precisely. Everyone is compelled to truth, no one is compelled to gnosis.

There is nothing more contradictory than a cerebral intelligence opposing itself to cardiac intelligence, whether it be to deny the possibility of knowledge or to deny the ultimate Knower: how can one not feel instinctively, "viscerally", existentially, that one cannot be intelligent, even very relatively so, without an Intelligence "in itself" that is both transcendent and immanent, and not grasp that subjectivity by itself is an immediate and quasi-fulgurating proof of the Omniscient, a proof almost too blindingly evident to be able to be formulated in words?

The intelligence of the heart is *a priori* the one which, all mental work notwithstanding, possesses the sense of the real, and thereby the sense of proportions as well; now to have the sense of the real is also, and even essentially, to have the sense of the sacred.

The intelligence comprises four functions: objectivity, subjectivity, activity, passivity; in the mind, these are reason, intuition, imagination, and memory. By "objectivity" we mean that knowledge is inspired by information which is external to it, and this is the role of reason; by "subjectivity", on the contrary, it must be understood that the knowledge in question operates through existential analogy, that is to say it is inspired by information which the subject bears within itself: hence we have no need of reasoning in order to observe the natural mechanism of a subjectivity foreign to us, and this is the faculty of intuition. In "activity", the intelligence relives, recreates, or combines the possibilities known to it, and this is the imagination; in "passivity", the intelligence registers and preserves information presenting itself to it. Since these four functions pertain to intelligence in itself—independently of the mental faculties we have enumerated—the intelligence communicates these functions to its so to speak feminine complement, sentiment, and to the will which extends both sentiment and intelligence.

In the macrocosm, "reason" is the order of things, whereas "intuition" is their symbolism and their providential intertwining; "imagination" is then the inexhaustible diversity of forms and destinies, and "memory", the persistence of possibilities throughout the vicissitudes of time and space.

It might be worth inserting a comment here that takes into consideration the fundamental human phenomenon constituted by the hierarchy of mental types: the contemplative or sacerdotal, the combative or princely, the practical or industrious, the obedient or loyal;[4] these qualities or predispositions, while strictly distinguishable, can always be combined, and they inevitably do so in indefinitely varied proportions. In each of these models, or within each of their combinations, are additionally situated the four temperaments and the twelve astrological types;[5] but all this is of a much more contingent order than the fundamental constitution of man—that of man as such—which opens out onto the divine order and has no meaning outside of it.

The spirit, we have said, is polarized into knowledge, love, and power, which permits the following question to be asked: what is the spirit in itself? The answer is given by the very elements of this polarization: the spirit—or the subject—is knowledge, not inasmuch as it looks "outward" and perceives "objects", but inasmuch as, bearing within itself its unique and total object, it looks "towards the Inward" and "extinguishes itself"—or on the contrary "realizes itself"—in the consciousness of its own one and indivisible substance. If we start from the idea that the object of knowledge is Truth or Reality; that the object of love is Beauty; and that the object of the will is the Good, then, starting from this idea or this premise, we could affirm that the spirit or the subject—which by definition knows, loves, and wills—is in its essence Truth, Beauty, and the Good.

---

[4] This last definition does not mean that the superior types would be devoid of loyalty, quite obviously, but that the fourth type—scarcely capable of governing himself—has *grosso modo* this one quality only, which constitutes his path as it were; and this of course to the extent that an individual is limited to this typological possibility.

[5] All told, men are differentiated by sex, age, temperament, zodiacal type, caste, and race.

The Absolute "radiates" by virtue of its intrinsic "dimension" of Infinitude, which brings about the "eruption" of *Māyā* that, for its part, both contains and produces reflections, worlds, beings: it is thus that one must distinguish a fundamental polarization within the human subject, namely the complementarity of spirit and soul, the first element belonging to the universal order, and the second constituting the individuality, hence the *Māyā* of the microcosm.

It has been said, quite paradoxically but not without reason, that the great mystery for the human spirit is Relativity rather than the Absolute; or *Māyā* rather than *Ātmā*. But one could also say, and more profoundly, that the mystery of mysteries is the internal Radiation of the Absolute; ungraspable Cause of the first Cause, and Cause without entering into any causal chain.

The Message of the Human Body

To say that man, and consequently the human body, is "made in the image of God" means *a priori* that it manifests something absolute and for that very reason something unlimited and perfect. What above all distinguishes the human form from animal forms is its direct reference to absoluteness, starting with its vertical posture; as a result, if animal forms can be transcended—and they are so by man, precisely—such could not be the case for the human form; this form marks not only the summit of earthly creatures, but also, and for this very reason, the exit from their condition, or from the *Samsāra* as Buddhists would say. To see man is to see not only the image of God, but also a door open towards *Bodhi*, liberating Enlightenment; or, let us say, towards a blessed centering in the divine Proximity.

Being absolute, the supreme Principle is *ipso facto* infinite; the masculine body accentuates the first aspect, and the feminine body the second. The divine Principle is, on the basis of these two hypostatic aspects, the source of all possible perfection; in other words, being the Absolute and the Infinite, It is necessarily also Perfection or the Good. Now each of the two bodies, the masculine and the feminine, manifests modes of perfection which their respective gender evokes by definition; all cosmic qualities are divided in fact into two complementary groups: the rigorous and the gentle, the active and the passive, the contractive and the expansive. The human body, as we have said, is an image of Deliverance: now the liberating Way may be either "virile" or "feminine", although it is not possible to have a strict line of demarcation between the two modes, for man (*homo, anthropos*) is always man; the non-material being that was the primordial androgyne survives in each of us.

This allusion to the primordial androgyne—which is divided in two well before the successive entry of its halves into matter[1]—permits us to make an ancillary comment. The human form cannot be transcended, its sufficient reason being precisely to express the Absolute, hence the unsurpassable; this cuts short the metaphysically and physically aberrant imaginings of the evolutionists, according to whom this form would

---

[1] And which is realized *a posteriori* in sexual union.

be the result of a prolonged elaboration starting from animal forms, an elaboration which is at once arbitrary and without end. Even materialists who consider that transformist evolution is unexplainable, not to say contradictory, accept this hypothesis as an indispensable idea, and this of course takes us outside of science and into philosophy, or more exactly into rationalism whose arguments are severed from the very roots of knowledge; and if the evolutionist idea is indispensable to these mate-rialists, it is because in their minds it replaces the concept of a sudden creation *ex nihilo*, which strikes them as being the only other possible solution. In reality, the evolutionist hypothesis is unnecessary because the creationist concept is so as well; for a creature appears on earth, not by falling from heaven, but by passing progressively—starting with its archetype—from the subtle world into the material world, its material-ization taking place within a kind of visible aura altogether comparable to the "spheres of light" that, according to many accounts, herald and terminate celestial apparitions.[2]

Quite clearly, deiformity essentially entails femininity, despite the opinion of certain ancient moralists who had difficulty reconciling the two; the one entails the other for simply logical as well as meta-physical reasons; even without knowing that femininity derives from an "Eternal Feminine" of a transcendent order, one is obliged to take account of the fact that woman, being situated like the male in the human state, is deiform because this state is deiform. Thus it is not surprising that a tradition as "misogynist" as Buddhism consented finally—within the *Mahāyāna* at least—to make use of the symbolism of the feminine body, which would be meaningless and even harmful if this body, or if femininity in itself, did not comprise a spiritual mes-sage of paramount importance; the Buddhas (and *Bodhisattvas*) do not save solely through doctrine, but also through their suprahuman beauty, according to the Tradition; now to speak of beauty is to speak implicitly of femininity; the beauty of the *Buddha* is necessarily that of *Māyā* or of *Tārā*.

---

[2] One will recall the "chariot of fire" that lifted up Elias, and the "cloud" which veiled the Christ during the Ascension.

The "misogyny" of Buddhism is explained by the fact that its method, at its origin and in general at least, appeals essentially to the characteristics of masculine psychology, which is to say that it operates basically with intellection, abstraction, negation, strength, and with what Amidism calls "power of oneself"; the same observation applies, if not to Hinduism as such, at least to certain of its schools and doubtless to its average perspective, which culminates, as in Buddhism, in the excessive and, to say the least, schematic idea that woman as such cannot attain Deliverance, that she must first be reborn in a masculine body and follow the methods of men. Ancient discussions on the question of knowing whether or not woman possesses a "soul" have a similar import: at issue was not the immortal soul, but the intellect in its most specifically masculine aspect. However that may be, the decisive point is not that woman has the concrete capacity to make use of specific methods, it is simply that, being human, she clearly has the capacity for sanctity.

But the anti-feminine ostracism of certain traditional perspectives has yet another cause than the question of qualification for a given yoga considered unique, and this is the idea that the male alone is the whole man. There are in fact two ways of situating the sexes, either in a horizontal or in a vertical sense: according to the first perspective, man is on the right and woman on the left; according to the second, man is above and woman below. On the one hand, man reflects *Ātmā* according to Absoluteness, and woman reflects it according to Infinitude; on the other hand, man alone is *Ātmā* and woman is *Māyā*;[3] but the second conception is relatively true only on condition that one also accepts the first; now the first conception takes precedence over the second, for the fact that woman is human clearly takes precedence over the fact that she is not a male.[4] The observation that specifically virile spiritual methods are scarcely suited to the feminine psychism becomes dogmatic in virtue of the second perspective which we

[3] There are passages in the various Scriptures which would allow one to believe that this is so, but which have to be understood in the light of other passages that remove their exclusiveness of style. As is well known, sacred Books proceed, not by means of nuanced formulations, but by antinomic affirmations; since it is impossible to accuse them of contradiction, it is necessary to draw the conclusions their antinomy requires.

[4] The *Shāstras* teach that women who serve their husbands by seeing in them their God, attain a masculine rebirth and thus attain Deliverance, which is obviously related to the maximal mode of the minimal possibility for woman.

have just mentioned; and the point could perhaps also be made that social conventions, in the traditional surroundings in question here, tend to create—at least on the surface—the feminine type that suits them ideologically and practically; humanity is so made that a social anthropology is never a perfect good, that it is on the contrary always a "lesser evil", or in any case an approximation.[5]

It is one of the paradoxes of Buddhism that even the Amidist way, although founded on Mercy and the "power of the Other"—not upon metaphysical meditation and the "power of oneself"—accepted, through pure conventionalism and without insisting thereon, this idea of woman having to be reborn as man; this is all the more perplexing in that the *Mahāyāna*—in its Tibetan form above all—has peopled its pantheon with feminine Divinities. The same paradox exists in Hinduism, *mutatis mutandis*, wherein one of the greatest personalities of Shivaism is a woman, Lalla Yogishwari; it is unthinkable that a "masculine body" would add anything whatsoever to her from the point of view of spiritual wholeness.[6]

What we have just said results moreover from the bodily form: first of all, the feminine body is far too perfect and spiritually too eloquent to be nothing more than a kind of transitory accident; and then, due to the fact that it is human, it communicates in its own way the same message as the masculine body, namely and to repeat, the absolutely Real and thereby the victory over the "round of births and deaths", hence the possibility of leaving the world of illusion and suffering. The animal, which can manifest perfections but not the Absolute, is like a closed door, enclosed as it were within its own per-

---

[5] As for Hinduism, it is appropriate to take into account the fact that, in this ambience, the concern for purity and the protection of sacred things is extreme, sacerdotal pedantism taking care of the rest; and it does so with respect to woman as well as to the categories of men deemed impure. Nonetheless, and this proves the prodigious "pluralism" of the Hindu spirit: "A mother is more venerable than a thousand fathers" (*Mānava Dharma Shāstra*, II, 145); and similarly, in Tantrism: "Whosoever sees the sole of a woman's foot, let him consider it as that of the spiritual master (*guru*)" (*Kubjika Tantra*).

[6] Let us also mention Maitreyi, wife of the *rishi* Yajnavalkya, who, according to the *Brihadāranyaka Upanishad*, "knew how to speak of *Brahma*," whereas the second wife of the sage "had scarcely more than the spirit of a woman"; and similarly the feminine *rishi*s Apala and Visvavara, both of whom revealed Vedic hymns; or the queen Chudala, wife and *guru* of the king Shikhidhwaja, who according to the *Yoga Vasishtha* had "realized *Ātmā*".

fection, whereas man is like an open door allowing him to escape his limits, which are those of the world rather than his own.

In an old book of legends, the chronicler who recounts an apparition of the Blessed Virgin with the Child Jesus observes that the Virgin was sublimely beautiful, but that the Child was "far more beautiful", which is absurd in more than one respect. First of all, there is no reason for the Child to be more beautiful than the Mother;[7] the divine nature possessed by the Child indeed requires perfect physical beauty, but the supereminent nature of the Virgin requires it equally as much; what the Christ possesses in addition to what is possessed by the Virgin could not determine a superior degree of beauty, given precisely that the beauty of the Virgin must be perfect; physical beauty belongs to the formal order, and form is by definition the manifestation of an archetype, the intention of which excludes an indefinite gradation. In other words, form coincides with an "idea" which cannot be something other than what it is; the human body has the form which characterizes it, and which it cannot transcend without ceasing to be itself; a beauty that can be indefinitely increased is meaningless, and empties the very notion of beauty of all its content. It is true that the mode or degree of divine Presence can add to the body, and above all to the face, an expressive quality, but this is independent of beauty in itself, which is a perfect theophany on its own plane; this is as much as to say that the theophanic quality of the human body resides uniquely in its form, and not in the sanctity of the soul inhabiting it nor, at the purely natural level, in the psychological beauty of an expression added to it, whether it be that of youth or of some noble sentiment.

Hence it is necessary to distinguish between the theophanic quality possessed by the human body in itself—beauty coinciding then with the wholeness and the intelligibility of this message—and the theophanic quality possessed in addition by this body in the case of the *Avatāra*s, such as Christ and the Virgin. In which case, as we have said, physical beauty must be perfect, and it may also be distinguished

---

[7] Which would imply that Mary would be "less beautiful" than Jesus, something inconceivable, because meaningless.

by an originality emphasizing its majesty; but the beauty of spiritual expression is of an altogether different order, and though it presupposes physical perfection and enhances it, it cannot however create it.

The body of the *Avatāra* is therefore sacred in a particular sense, one that is supereminent and so to speak sacramental by virtue of its quasi-divine content; however the ordinary body is also sacred, but in an altogether different respect, simply because it is human; in addition, physical beauty is sacred because it manifests the divine Intention for that body, and thus is fully itself according to its regularity and nobility.[8]

There is not only the beauty of the adult, there is also that of the child as our reference of the Child Jesus suggests. First of all, it must be said that the child, being human, participates in the same symbolism and in the same aesthetic expressivity as his parents—we are speaking always of man as such and not of particular individuals—and then, that childhood is nevertheless a provisional state and does not in general have the definitive and representative value of maturity.[9] In metaphysical symbolism, this provisional character expresses relativity: the child is what "comes after" his parents; he is the reflection of *Ātmā* in *Māyā*, at one degree or another and according to the ontological or cosmological level in view; or the child is even *Māyā* itself if the adult is *Ātmā*.[10] But from an altogether different standpoint, and according to inverse analogy, the key to which is given by the seal of Solomon,[11]

---

[8] Let it be said in passing that this is totally independent of questions of race: every race, excepting more or less degenerate groups—although even a collective degeneration does not necessarily exclude cases of individual beauty—comprises modes of perfect beauty, each expressing a fundamental aspect of human theophany in itself.

[9] Although it can when the individual worth of the child visibly takes precedence over his state of immaturity; nevertheless, childhood is in itself an incomplete state pointing towards its own completion.

[10] Polarized into "Necessary Being" and "All-Possibility".

[11] When a tree is mirrored in a lake, its top is at the bottom, but the image is always that of a tree; the analogy is inverse in the first relationship and parallel in the second. Analogies between the divine order and the cosmic order always comprise one or the other of these relationships.

the child represents on the contrary what "was before", namely what is simple, pure, innocent, primordial, and close to the Essence, and this is what its beauty expresses;[12] this beauty has all the charm of promise, of hope, and of blossoming, and at the same time that of a Paradise not yet lost; it combines the proximity of the Origin with the striving towards the Goal. For this reason childhood constitutes a necessary aspect of integral man, hence a being in conformity with the divine Intention: the man who has attained his human fullness always keeps—in perfect balance with wisdom—the qualities of simplicity and freshness, of gratitude and trust, which he possessed in the spring-time of his life.[13]

Since we have just mentioned the principle of inverse analogy, we can take note here of its application to femininity: even though femininity is *a priori* subordinate to virility, it also comprises an aspect which makes it superior to a given aspect of the masculine pole, for the divine Principle has an aspect of limitlessness, virginal mystery, and maternal mercy which takes precedence over a certain more relative aspect of determination, logical precision, and implacable justice.[14] Seen thus, feminine beauty appears as an initiatic wine in the face of the rationality represented in certain respects by the masculine body.[15]

A priori, virility refers to the Principle, and femininity to Manifestation; but in an altogether different respect, that of complementarity *in divinis*, the masculine body expresses Transcendence, and

[12] We do not say that every human individual is beautiful when he is a child, but we start from the idea that man, whether a child or not, is beautiful to the extent that he is physically what he ought to be.

[13] "Verily I say unto you, except ye be converted, and become as little children, ye shall not enter into the Kingdom of Heaven" (Matt. 18:3).

[14] According to Tacitus, the Germanic tribes perceived something sacred and visionary in women. The fact that in German the sun (*die Sonne*) is feminine whereas the moon (*der Mond*) is masculine, testifies to the same perspective.

[15] Mahayanic art represents *Prajnāpāramitā*, the "Perfection of Gnosis", in feminine form; likewise, *Prajnā*, liberating Knowledge, appears as a woman by contrast with *Upāya*, the doctrinal system or the art of persuading, which is depicted as masculine. The Buddhists readily point out that the *Bodhisattvas*, asexual in themselves, have the power to take a feminine form as they do any other form; now one would like to know for what reason they do so, for if the feminine form can produce such a great good, it is because it is intrinsically good; otherwise there would be no reason for a *Bodhisattva* to assume it.

the feminine body, Immanence; Immanence being close to Love, and Transcendence to Knowledge.

Much could be said about the abstract and concrete symbolism of the different regions or parts of the body. A symbolism is abstract inasmuch as it signifies a principial reality; it is concrete inasmuch as it communicates the nature of this reality, that is, inasmuch as it makes it present to our experience. One of the most striking characteristics of the human body is the breast, which is a solar symbol, the accentuation differing according to sex: noble and glorious radiation in both male and female, but manifesting power in the first case and generosity in the second—the power and generosity of pure Being.[16] The heart is the center of man, and the breast is so to speak the face of the heart; and since the heart-intellect comprises both Knowledge and Love, it is plausible that in the human body this polarization manifests itself by the complementarity of the masculine and feminine breasts.

The human body comprises three fundamental regions: the body properly so-called, the head, the sexual parts; these are almost three different subjectivities. The head represents a subjectivity that is at once intellectual and individual; the body, a collective and archetypal subjectivity, that of masculinity or femininity or that of race or caste; finally, the sexual parts manifest, quite paradoxically, a dynamic subjectivity at once animal and divine, if one may express it thus. In other words, the face expresses a thought, an awareness, a truth; the body, for its part, expresses a being, an existential synthesis; and the sexual parts, a love both creative and liberating: mystery of the generous substance that unfolds in the form of accidents, and of the blessed accidents that flow back towards the substance; glory of self-giving and glory of delivering. The human body, considered as a whole, is intelligence, existence, love; certitude, serenity, and faith.

One of the functions of dress is, no doubt, to isolate mental subjectivity—the subjectivity that thinks and speaks—from the two existential subjectivities which risk disturbing the message of thought with their own messages; nonetheless this is a question of tempera-

[16] The ritual dance of the dervishes—setting aside the variety of its forms—is often designated by the term *dhikr as-sadr*, "remembrance (of God) by the breast", which evokes this verse of the Koran: "Have We (God) not expanded thy breast?" (*Sūrah* "Solace" [94]:1). Koranic language moreover establishes a relationship between the acceptance of Islam—as "resignation" or "abandon" (*islām*) to the divine Will—and dilation of the breast; calm and deep respiration expressing truth, peace, happiness.

ment and custom, for a man who is still more or less primordial has in this respect reflexes other than those of a man who is overly marked by the fall—namely, of a creature become at once too cerebral and too passional, and having lost much of his beauty and also his innocence.

The gait of the human being is as evocative as his vertical posture; whereas the animal is horizontal and only advances towards itself—for it is enclosed within its own form—man, in advancing, transcends himself; even his forward movement seems vertical, it denotes a pilgrimage towards his Archetype, towards the celestial Kingdom, towards God. The beauty of the anterior side of the human body indicates the nobleness, on the one hand of man's vocational end, and on the other hand of his manner of approaching it; it indicates that man is moving towards God and that he does so in a manner that is "humanly divine", one might say. However the posterior side of the body also has its meaning: it indicates, the noble innocence of the origin, on the one hand and, on the other, the noble manner of leaving behind ourselves what has been transcended; it expresses, positively, whence we have come and, negatively, how we turn our backs to what is no longer ourselves. Man comes from God and he goes towards God; but at the same time, he draws away from an imperfection that is no longer his own and draws nearer to a perfection that is not yet his. His "becoming" bears the imprint of a "being"; he is that which he becomes, and he becomes that which he is.

—— ·:· ——

It was necessary to allude earlier to the evolutionist error given our considerations on the deformity of man, and this enables us to insert a parenthetical comment here. The animal, vegetal, and mineral species not only manifest qualities or combinations of qualities, they also manifest defects or combinations of defects, for this is required by All-Possibility, which short of being limited—namely of not being what it is—must also express "possible impossibilities", or let us say negative and paradoxical possibilities; therefore it implies excess as well as privation and, in so doing, enhances by means of contrasts what the norm is. In this respect, the ape for example is there to show both what man is and what he is not, but certainly not what he has been; far from being able to be a virtual form of man, the ape incarnates an animal desire to be human, hence a desire of imitation and usurpation; but it finds itself as it were before a closed door and falls back all the more heavily into its animality, the perfect innocence of which, however, it can no longer recapture, if one may use such a metaphor; it is as if the animal, prior to the creation of man and to protest against it, had wished to anticipate it, which evokes the refusal of Lucifer to bow down before Adam.[17] This does not prevent the ape from being sacred in India, perhaps on account of its anthropomorphism, or more likely because of associations of ideas connected to an extrinsic symbolism;[18] this would also explain in part the role played by the apes in the *Rāmāyana*, unless we are dealing in this case with subtle creatures—the *jinn* of Islam—of whom the ape would be only a likeness.[19]

One may wonder whether the intrinsically noble animals, those possessing an immediately positive symbolism, are not themselves theophanies as well; they are so necessarily, and the same holds true for given plants, minerals, cosmic, or terrestrial phenomena, but in these cases the theomorphism is partial and not integral as in man. The splendor of the stag excludes that of the lion, the eagle cannot be the swan, nor the water lily the rose, nor the emerald the sapphire; from a somewhat different point of view, we could say that the sun manifests the divine Majesty in a direct and simple manner, but that it has neither life nor spirit;[20] man alone is the image-synthesis of the Creator,[21] owing to the fact that he possesses the intellect—hence also reason and language—and that he manifests it by his very form.

[17] According to the *Talmud* and the Koran.

[18] As was the case for the boar, which represents sacerdotal authority for the Nordics; or as the rhinoceros symbolizes the *sannyāsī*.

[19] The story recounted in the *Rāmāyana* is situated at the end of the "silver age" (*Tretā-Yuga*) and consequently in a climate of possibilities quite different from that of the "iron age" (*Kali-Yuga*); the partition between the material and animic states was not yet "hardened" or "congealed" as is especially the case in our epoch.

[20] It can nevertheless have a sacramental function for men who are sensitive to cosmic *barakah*.

[21] And this in spite of the loss of the earthly Paradise. One of the effects of what mono-theist symbolism calls the "fall of Adam", was the separation between the soul and the body, conjointly with the separation between heaven and earth and between the spirit and the soul. The "resurrection of the flesh" is none other than the restoration of the primordial situation; given that the body is an immanent virtuality of the soul,

— ∴ —

Let us now return to the question of traditional misogynist view-points. Buddhism, as we already noted, is essentially a masculine, abstract, negative, ascetic, and heroic spirituality, at least *a priori* and in its broad outlines; hence the feminine body must appear to it as the embodiment *par excellence* of seduction and thereby of *samsāra*, of the round of births and deaths. But we are here in the presence of that inverse analogy which we referred to above: in this case what draws downwards is what, in reality, is situated above; and femininity, inasmuch as it seduces and binds, has this aspect precisely because it offers—in itself and in the intention of the Creator—an image of lib-erating Bliss; now a reflection is always "something" of what it reflects, which amounts to saying that it "is" this reality in an indirect mode and on the plane of contingency. This is what the Buddhists grasped in the framework of Mahayanic esoterism—the Tibetans and the Mongols above all—and it is this which permitted them to introduce nude *Tārās* and *Dākinīs*, in gilded bronze, into their sanctuaries; the corporeal theophany of feminine type is intended to actualize in the faithful the remembrance of the merciful and beatific dimension of *Bodhi* and of *Nirvāna*.

What is true for a certain Buddhism is true *a priori* for Hinduism, the sacred art of which exposes and accentuates the message of both human bodies, the masculine and the feminine: message of ascending and unitive verticality in both cases, certainly, but in rigorous, tran-scendent, objective, abstract, rational, and mathematical mode in the first case, and in gentle, immanent, concrete, emotional, and musical mode in the second. On the one hand, there is a path centered on the metaphysical Idea and on Rigor, and on the other hand, a path centered on the sacramental Symbol and on Gentleness—not to men-tion diverse combinations of the two perspectives, temperaments, or methods, for the absolute male cannot exist anymore than can the absolute female, given that there is but one sole *anthropos*. Thus, there are spiritualities, and even religions, which could be qualified as "femi-nine", without this character signifying that their adepts lose anything

it can be remanifested as soon as the separative "curse" has drawn to its close, which coincides with the end of a great cycle of humanity.

whatever of their virility;[22] and the converse is just as true, for there have been women in paths which are the least representative of their mentality; both possibilities seem sufficiently obvious so as to dispense us from having to explore all the twists and turns of this paradox.

One may wonder why the Hindus, and still more so the Buddhists, did not fear to provide occasions for a fall in their sacred art, given that beauty—sexual beauty above all—invites to "let go of the prey for its shadow", that is, to forget the transcendent content through being attached to the earthly husk. Now it is not for nothing that Buddhist art, more than any other, has given voice to the fearful aspects of cosmic manifestation; at the very least this constitutes a "reestablishing of the balance": for the spectator is warned never to lose sight of the menace of the pitiless *samsāra* everywhere present, nor that of the Guardians of the Sanctuary. *Darshan*—the contemplation of the Divine in nature or in art—quite clearly presupposes a contemplative temperament; now it is this very temperament that comprises a sufficient guarantee against the attitude of casualness and of profanation.

The morality and mysticism of the West see in concupiscence nothing but carnal sin, but this is a one-sided and insufficient perspective; in reality, sin lies here just as much in the profanation of a theophanic mystery; it consists in the fact of pulling downwards, towards the frivolous and the trivial that which by its nature points upwards and towards the sacred; but sin or deviation can also be found—at a level not deprived of nobility in this instance—in the purely aesthetic and individualistic cult of the body, as was the case in classical Greece, where the sense of clarity, of measure, of finite perfection, had completely obliterated the sense of the transcendent, of mystery, and of the infinite. Sensible beauty became an end in itself; it was no longer man who resembled God, it was God who resembled man; whereas in Egyptian and Hindu art, which express the substantial and not the accidental, one feels that the human form is nothing without a mystery which fashions it on the one hand and, on the other, transcends it, and which calls both to Love and to Deliverance.

---

[22] In Krishnaism, the masculine adepts consider themselves as *gopīs*, lovers of Krishna, which is all the more plausible in that with respect to the Divinity every creature has something feminine about it.

The Sense of the Sacred

One of the most immediately intelligible and convincing outward signs of Islam is the call to prayer from the top of the minarets; it is a call that spreads like a blanket of serenity over the souls of the believers, from dawn and all the way into the night. Here we are far from scholastic arguments, yet there is an argument nonetheless: to be precise, a "sign", that is to say an argument appealing, not to conceptual intelligence, but to aesthetic intuition and, more fundamentally, to the sense of the sacred.

As with intellectual discernment, the sense of the sacred is an adequation to the Real, with the difference however, that the knowing subject is then the entire soul and not merely the discriminative intelligence. What the intelligence perceives quasi-mathematically, the soul senses in an as it were musical manner that is both moral and aesthetic; it is immobilized and at the same time vivified by the message of blessed eternity that the sacred transmits.

The sacred is the projection of the celestial Center into the cosmic periphery, or of the "Motionless Mover" into the flux of things. To feel this concretely is to possess the sense of the sacred, and thereby the instinct of adoration, devotion, and submission; the sense of the sacred is the awareness—within the world of that which may or may not be—of That which cannot not be, whose immense remoteness and miraculous proximity we experience at one and the same time. The reason such an awareness is possible for us is because necessary Being reaches us in the depth of our heart, through a mystery of immanence that makes us capable of knowing all that is knowable, and which for that very reason makes us immortal.

The sense of the sacred is also the innate consciousness of the presence of God:[1] it is to feel this presence sacramentally in symbols and ontologically in all things.[2] Hence the sense of the sacred entails a kind

---

[1] It is to this consciousness of the divine presence which the well-known *hadīth* on *ihsān* refers: "Perfect piety (*ihsān* = "right action") is that you adore God as if you were seeing Him, and if you do not see Him, He nonetheless sees you."

[2] The reverential tendency resulting therefrom is readily termed "pantheism", while forgetting on the one hand that this term designates merely the reduction of the Divine

of universal respect, a kind of deferential reserve before the mystery of animate and inanimate creatures, but at the same time without either any unduly favorable prejudice or any weakness towards phenomena that demonstrate errors or vices, and, because of this, that no longer present any mystery unless it be that of the absurd. Such phenomena are metaphysically necessary, no doubt, but they represent in fact an absence of the sacred, and thus play a negative role in our respect for existence, operating by way of contrast; this notwithstanding, the pious and contemplative soul feels a natural respect for the things nature surrounds us with.

There is in the sacred an aspect of rigor, invincibility, and inviolability, and an aspect of gentleness, appeasement, and mercy; a mode of riveting fascination and a mode of liberating attraction. The devotional spirit must express both characteristics; it cannot stop short at fear alone, which moreover would be incompatible with the nature of contemplation. Majesty can be the object of contemplation only by virtue of the presence within it of an element of appeasing beauty or serenity, and this emanates more particularly from the dimension of Infinitude proper to the Absolute.

The sacred is the projection of the Immutable into the mutable; as a result, the sense of the sacred consists not only in perceiving this projection, but also in detecting in things the trace of the Immutable, to the point of not letting oneself be deceived and enslaved by the mutable. This is how the experience of beauty must be lived so as to draw from it a lasting and not ephemeral element, hence by realizing in oneself an opening towards immutable Beauty, rather than plunging into the current of things; it is a question of viewing the world, and living in it, in a manner that is sacred and not profane; or sacralizing and not profaning. This brings us back once again to the mystery of the twofold aspect of *Māyā*, the *Māyā* that imprisons and the one that delivers.[3]

---

to the visible world, and on the other hand that God is truly immanent in the world— otherwise the world could not exist—in varying degrees and without detriment to His rigorous transcendence.

[3] The first being at the same time the one that disperses, and the second, the one that unifies.

Let us now consider our subject in its secondary and practical aspects. The sense of the sacred, by the very fact that it coincides with devotion, essentially implies dignity: firstly moral dignity, the virtues, and then dignity of bearing, of gesture; external comportment, which belongs to the moving periphery, must bear witness to the "Motionless Center".[4] Thus the sacred evokes, rightly or wrongly, the image of solemnity, of grave and slow gestures, of complicated and interminable rituals; wrongly so, in that the sacred is not bound to forms, although it excludes those which are incompatible with its nature; and rightly so, given that the sacred indeed transposes the immutable or the eternal into movement or the temporal.

It is a fact that ceremonialism, like ritualism, derives from the sense of the sacred, either directly and legitimately, or indirectly and by caricature. It is possible to speak of the ritualism of a religion as such, for ceremonies come from men, fairly or abusively: fairly, for the ceremonies surrounding a prince derive from the sacred character of his person, since he is a prince "by the grace of God", and this is proved by his anointment; abusively, because republican ceremonies, for example, are nothing but counterfeits without authority or reality.[5]

Legitimate ceremonies derive most often from historical incidents that create "precedents"; they derive from an inspiration which could be qualified as "ethnic" given that the racial or cultural soul has a right, not to the creation of rites of course, but to the manifestation of its sacral sensibility in the form of ceremonies and other elements of the kind. This right extends even into the religious domain in the sense that ceremonies often form the framework of rites: even within the religious domain, the collective soul preserves its rights, on the plane which corresponds to them and not beyond. This is quite apparent in

---

[4] According to a *hadīth*, "Slowness comes from God and haste comes from the devil." Now the first relates to the sense of the sacred, and the second to the profane spirit, roughly speaking and without excluding reverse modes; there are cases wherein the Holy Spirit inspires to swiftness and the devil incites to slowness.

[5] The unavowed intention in cases of this kind is to attribute a sacred character to profane things, which is all the more abusive in that the promoters of the profane deny the sacred as such.

Hinduism, where it is sometimes difficult to separate the ceremonial from the ritual; and even in Christianity, which is however less luxuriant, the two elements at times appear to be mingled in the liturgy; assuredly, there is no confusion, but the rite seems to require imperiously, and as a *conditio sine qua non,* some ceremonial complement.

The efficacy of rites is objective; that of ceremonies is subjective; rites communicate graces which pre-exist outside of us, whereas ceremonies contribute towards actualizing our receptivity, either simply by stimulating the pious imagination, or, more profoundly, by appealing to "Platonic recollection". When Saint Basil declares, in speaking of ritual words, that "we add others before and after to lend greater power to the mysteries", he has in view the human receptivity only, not the divine efficaciousness, hence the subjective import of the ceremonial element, not the objective import of the rite.[6]

Clearly, the secondary sources of the sacral mentality differ from one religion to another. In Christianity the sacred emanates from the sacrament, which confers upon the collective sense of the sacred its characteristic style, notably the taste for solemnity, without forgetting the splendor of the liturgical art, such as the iconostases, the golden retables, and the priestly vestments. In Islam, where there are no sacraments properly so called, the collective piety has a strongly obediential quality: to be pious, is above all to obey—with bowed head and without concern for the why of things—the Koranic and Muhammadan injunctions; it is also the taste for interminable prayers and mystical litanies to the glory of the Prophet, all of which takes us back, by analogy, to the holy ponderousness of the Christian liturgy. Adapted to collectivities, the sense of the sacred gives rise to amplifications which we could designate as "indispensable abuses": collective piety seems to require a kind of mortification by means of a solemn prolixity, as far removed as possible from the haste-driven trivialities

---

[6] This is true *a fortiori* when it is a question of outward signs, such as genuflections, the swinging of censers, the tinkling of the bells, which we cannot object to for the simple reason that these are, strictly speaking, ceremonies and not rites. In many instances, the ceremony is to the rite what clothing is to the body.

of profane life, and yet equally removed from sapiential serenity; thus pure wisdom, which is neither groveling nor irreverent, has no easy life in such a climate, and esoteric literature shows the effects of it, in Islam perhaps more than anywhere else.

But let us return to the sacred and to the sacral mentality in itself: in Hinduism, the one as well as the other is manifested most characteristically by the ritual gestures of the hands, the *mūdra*s, which are found in *Mahāyāna* Buddhism as well; for the Hindus, there is also an essentializing relationship between the sacred and nudity, which Buddhism did not retain except for the images of celestial beings. In Buddhism, the visible and tactile sacred has its basis above all in the images—especially the statues—of the Buddha, and by projection, of the *Bodhisattva*s, the *Tārā*s, and other quasi-divine realities; this art attained summits of perfection and interiorizing expressivity with the Tibeto-Mongols on the one hand and the Japanese on the other hand. The extinction of form in the Essence requires as a counterpart the manifestation of the Essence in form: whether through the image as in Buddhism, or through the theomorphic human body as in Hinduism, or again through the eucharistic liturgy—including the icon—in Christianity. Let us also mention the verbal theophany which is the psalmodized recitation of the revealed texts, calligraphy being its visual mode; or again, in Islam, the canonical prayer, the majestic movement of which expresses the sacred in a manner that from the point of view in question is not unrelated to the *mūdra*s of India.

We alluded above to what we have termed the "indispensable abuses" of sacrality in the face of collective mentalities. Before criticizing a given problematical and at first glance irrational phenomenon in a religion, one must ask the following general question: how does a religion succeed in effectively and durably imposing the sense of the sacred upon a large human collectivity? And one must take account of the fact that in order to achieve this result, it must tolerate or even favor certain excesses which, in practice, are inevitable and conform to its general style; many things which, in religions, may seem excessive to us, or even absurd, fundamentally have the merit of replacing the vices of the profane mind and of contributing in their own way to the sense of the sacred; all of which is too easily lost sight of and which in any case constitutes an "attenuating circumstance", and not among the least.

This is not to say that the sacred coincides in an absolute manner with the traditional in the strict sense of the word: that is "traditional" which is transmitted from a divine source; now, while this divine source does not manifest, we say, outside of the traditional framework, it can do so independently of inherited formulations, otherwise there would be neither inspiration nor diversity of schools. In other words, there is in the sacred a "vertical" and discontinuous manifestation as well as a "horizontal" and continuous manifestation; and this is all the more true when it is a question of intellectuality, hence of essentiality and universality.

Within the framework of a traditional civilization, intellectuality as well as art have the possibility and consequently the right to be original, on express condition that the originality be the fruit of an inspiration and not of a desire; the prejudice in favor of "creativity" excludes *a priori* all participation of the Holy Spirit. Inspiration is something which by definition imposes itself without our expecting it, although our nature must be predisposed to it; David was the last to want to be king, but it is he who was chosen.

There is nothing paradoxical in the idea that man cannot be a metaphysician in the full sense without possessing the sense of the sacred; Plotinus is certainly not the only one to have pointed this out. The reason for this is not that the intelligence cannot *a priori* perceive the true without the assistance of moral qualities, but that by itself it is not capable of excluding all possibility of error, given that errors often have their source in the imperfection of the soul, for man is a whole; it is no less true that, beyond a certain level of perception, the intelligence has need of special graces that largely depend upon moral qualification in the broadest sense of the term. Incontestably, moral and aesthetic sensibility—which is not a luxury since it forms part of the human norm—influences to one degree or another the formulation of transcendent truths, and even above all the speculative imagination and its requisite sense of proportions. In an altogether general manner, we would say that one cannot enter the sanctuary of truth except in a holy manner, and this condition includes above all beauty of character, which is inseparable from the sense of the sacred.

The two poles of the sacred are truth and holiness: truth and holiness of persons and of things. A thing is true by its symbolism and holy by the depth of its beauty; all beauty is a cosmic mode of holiness. In the spiritual order, man is in the truth through his knowledge, and he is holy through his personal conformity to the truth and through the depth of this conformity.

In principle, truth and holiness cannot contradict each other; nonetheless, in the domain of traditional orthodoxy, conflicts between the sense of the sacred and the critical sense, or between piety and intelligence, are always possible, because either piety can be manifested in intellectually inferior modalities or else the same can happen with intelligence; sentimentalism is not mystical love, any more than intellectualism is intellectuality. One could debate the question of intelligence all day long, at least so long as one does not see clearly that intelligence is defined essentially by its capacity to grasp the object, and only secondarily by its subjective qualities, those of expression, logic, the combination of ideas and so on; this should go without saying. If we consider subjectivity according to its positive reality, we can say that subjective intelligence accentuates the modes of assimilation of the object, whereas objective intelligence focuses upon the object as such; there is also an intelligence that is concrete and another that is abstract, and other complementarities such as activity and passivity, discernment and contemplation; but it is always adequation, hence truth, which takes precedence over the secondary modes.

It is all too evident that fundamental intelligence is manifested, not in the fact of accepting lofty ideas, but by the capacity to really understand them, even if one rejects them accidentally either due to a lack of information or because the medium of information *de facto* lacks intelligibility. There are people, whether intelligent or not, who adopt transcendent ideas out of ambition; however it is a fact that people of modest intelligence often accept such ideas more readily than others of brilliant intelligence, or are nimbler in accepting them, whether this be thanks to a contemplative instinct or simply thanks to the absence of intellectual scruples, or for both reasons. But whatever might be the degree of intelligence, incomprehension does not necessarily stem from a fundamental limitation of the mind; its cause may also be a moral tendency of the soul; it remains to be seen to what degree this tendency is personal or is on the contrary imposed by the surroundings. If we compare a religious believer who is closed to a given esoteric idea because of his faith, with another man who, without being more intelligent than the former—he may even be much less so—adopts the same idea out of mere vanity, the question which then arises is that of knowing whether holding a sublime idea for insincere motives is really equivalent to a knowledge. No doubt there is a faint trace of mental knowledge, but it is condemned in advance to sterility, precisely because it has no connection with the sense of the sacred—the sacred, which requires fear as well as love. For extremes meet, and the circle which opens in truth closes in beauty.

It might perhaps, in this general context, be worthwhile to speak about miracles, which are essentially a manifestation and, if one will, a proof of the sacred, whence the catalyzing power they have upon souls. As in the case of the sacred in general, the chief argument here is based upon the reality of the supernatural and, by way of consequence, upon the necessity for the eruption of the supernatural into the natural order. It is necessary first of all to be in agreement as to the meaning of the word "supernatural": the supernatural can be what is contrary to the laws of nature, but it cannot be what is contrary to the very principles of the Universe; if we term "natural" that which simply obeys the logic of things, without restrictions, the supernatural is also natural, but it is so on a scale far vaster than that of physical causality, that of this lower world. The supernatural is the "divinely natural" which, irrupting into an eminently contingent and limited plane of the natural, contradicts the laws of this plane, not by virtue of the causality proper to the latter, of course, but by virtue of a causality that is far less contingent and limited. If "God exists"—really and fully, and not as some unconscious and passive "power" as the naturalists and deists would have it—then miracles cannot not be; transcendence as well as immanence require that this mode of theophany have its place in the economy of things possible.

The problem of miracles is essentially linked to the doctrine of possibility; depending upon whether a man is ignorant or informed, opaque or intuitive, he will wonder whether miracles are possible or what is the explanation of their possibility; the metaphysician in any case cannot ignore that universal Possibility implies and requires the apparent paradox of the miraculous intervention. A miracle is like sunrise: it pre-exists in the divine order and it manifests only in conjunction with a human opening; thus the sun rises because the earth turns towards it, whereas in reality the sun is fixed in relation to the earth. Nature is like a moving veil before an immutable supernature.

In the cosmogonic order, the miracle is prefigured by the eruption of life into matter, and all the more so by the eruption of intelligence both into matter and into life; the human species would be the quintessential miracle if the notion of the miraculous could be applied in such a case. On this plane of the "human miracle", the eruption of Revelation constitutes yet another miracle; and the same is true for Intellection and for all other incidental interventions of the Holy Spirit. For what is true for the macrocosm is equally true for the microcosm: if the miraculous exists outwardly, then it also exists inwardly. The microcosmic or inward miracle is that which manifests the divine Presence in the soul: gnosis, ecstasy, the sacrament, sanctity, all of which furnish so many proofs of the possibility, as well as of the necessity, of an unimaginable eruption of the divine element; and what is possible within ourselves is possible around us.

When speaking of miracles as such, one must also take account, if not of all their modes and of all their forms, which is scarcely possible, but of the causes of their frequency or, on the contrary, of their scarceness; for not every miracle is possible in every epoch or in every situation. It is in the nature of things that the unfolding of a religion be accompanied by a proliferation of wonders that lasts for a millennium or so, only to dwindle more and more until their near extinction towards the end of the religious cycle, and without it being possible to draw clear dividing lines within this process. And miracles become more and more rare not only because of the progressive hardening of the psychic and physical substance of the world, but also because of the hardening of hearts, both causes going hand in hand and determining one another mutually and by alternations. Between matter and the animic element a "layer of ice" forms, which isolates matter more and more by cutting it off from the subtle world that surrounds and penetrates it; skepticism provokes the silence of Heaven, and this silence favors skepticism. And within the human microcosm itself, the soul becomes separated from the spirit and the spirit closes itself to the soul.

The character trait termed "credulity" or the "thirst for the marvelous" can be explained by the innumerable experiences of miraculous occurrences over many thousands of years, but which have become more and more precarious; these experiences, quite naturally, have left in the collective soul the nostalgia for a paradise which is slipping away but whose loss one does not wish to acknowledge, all the more so in that, precisely, it is not wholly lost, and that, against all hope, it reappears from time to time. Parallel to the effusion of miraculous incidents—the style of which varies moreover from one religion to another—one detects, especially when reading the Oriental hagiographers, a collective sensibility unknown in our times and hard to imagine;[7] certainly, there is also the creative imagination of legends, but this phenomenon cannot invalidate what we have just said for the simple reason that if many accounts cannot be taken literally, there are many others which incontestably can, beginning with historical texts such as the Gospels and the Acts of the Apostles, and which precede and determine the legends. And this is independent of the fact that, in the sacred Scriptures, certain wondrous occurrences have a symbolic character only, at least when dealing with more or less "prehistoric" events, the symbolical character of which is readily recognized.[8]

The difference between preaching about God and a miracle that manifests Him is, all told, that between the word and the thing denoted,

---

[7] Men cry out, faint, fall into ecstasy, sometimes die, under the effect of a given manifestation of *barakah*, sometimes even following a particularly enlightening or striking formulation.

[8] Such is notably the case of Biblical stories up to and including that of the Tower of Babel, stories which can be termed "myths" without the slightest pejorative intention. What is particular to the myth is that on the one hand its meaning takes precedence over the facts, and that on the other hand it also applies to the life of the soul, at the initiatic level as well as the simply moral level.

or between abstract doctrine and its concrete content: by the miracle, God says "I am here", whereas preaching is limited to affirming that God is. It is in fact impossible that a God, who on the one hand is absent and who on the other hand wants to be known and must be known, never make Himself present, at least in a way that His nature permits and that the world can bear; and similarly in the soul: it is impossible that a reality perceived indirectly by thought, and yet that is intellectually compelling in the manner of a "categorical imperative", never be perceived directly by the heart, thus proving as it were its truth by its presence and by its existence, hence through experience.

This perception by the heart is realized not only by gnosis, which is unitive by definition, but also by faith, which *a priori* remains separate from its object; the mystery of faith is in fact the possibility of an anticipatory perception in the absence of its content; that is, faith makes present its content by accepting it already, before the perception properly so-called. And if faith is a mystery, it is because its nature is inexpressible in the measure that it is profound, for it is not possible to convey fully by words this vision which is still blind, and this blindness which already sees.

To Refuse or To Accept Revelation

Many Koranic stories present to us, with even more insistence than the Bible, the following motif: the prophets preach and the people reject the Message; God punishes them for this rejection; and He rewards those men who believe.

The objection of agnostics and other skeptics is too facile: different peoples are psychologically excusable for not accepting the Messages; the pagan Arabs had the right, humanly and even traditionally, to believe in the reality of their divinities and in the efficacy of their idols; they had no reason for believing the Prophet as opposed to their traditions and their customs. Even miracles, where applicable, cannot constitute a proof, given the wonders of magic. It is true that the moderns deny these wonders as well as miracles, but we mention the argument nevertheless since, in the opinion of the moderns, miracles would prove nothing "if they existed", since they can be imitated.[1] Similarly, it has been said over and over that the Pharisees had no reason for accepting the message of Christ, that on the contrary they had reasons for not accepting it; this is partly true and partly false, taking into account the intrinsic orthodoxy of Mosaism on the one hand and on the other hand the prophetic quality of Christ.

Regarding the pagan Arabs, the excuse of the moderns—easy enough on the part of people who believe in nothing and who are unaware of the plenary nature of man—this excuse, we say, does not take into account the following factor: if the majority of Meccans and Bedouins obstinately held on to their customs, this was not *a priori* for sincere and logical reasons, but fundamentally because their so-called religion, which did not even teach them the indispensable eschatological truths, on the contrary flattered their passionate attachment to the here-below and their chaotic and even exclusive love for earthly goods.[2] And it is precisely this attachment and this love which

---

[1] Which is not the case, strictly speaking, for the miracle requires a context which in reality makes it inimitable, otherwise it would have no reason for existing; besides, magic is far from being able to counterfeit all miracles, so much so that the argument in question is exceedingly weak.

[2] "When Our verses (the Koran) are recited before him (the pagan Arab), he says:

prevented them from admitting from the outset that the Prophet was no ordinary man and that the doctrine of divine Unity and human immortality deserved the highest consideration at the very least; and it prevented them from sensing that this Message is inscribed in the very substance of the heart.

In the face of the Message of Truth, man could not legitimately raise the question of credibility if he were not himself a form of truth, hence of conformity to the True. One cannot examine the Truth in a valid manner on the basis of error, nor the sacred on the basis of the profane; one cannot judge the Message outside of a disposition that anticipates it and that manifests the deiform and hence primordial nature of man. Religions differ in the way they envisage and express the two fundamental truths, namely God and immortality, but not in their unanimous function of detaching man from the here-below and from the ego in order to lead him toward the hereafter and towards the Divine. If some psychologists so-called agree with the ancient pagans, it is because they recognize themselves in them; but they understand the situation of these pagans as little as they understand their own.

The man for whom the Message is providentially destined[3] must recognize in it what is best in himself; he cannot escape intellectually and morally the truth of this call any more than he can escape existentially the reality of his heart.

In all of these considerations, it is a question *a priori* of the confrontation between the founders of religion or their direct delegates and of men adhering either to outright paganisms or to religions that are debilitated or disfigured, at least sporadically; it is not in principle a question of the confrontation between Apostles and Pythagorean initiates, for example, nor between civilizationist missionaries and primi-

---

fables of the ancients!" (*Sūrah* "The Pen" [68]:15). This information, which the Koran furnishes several times, proves that the religion of the pagan Arabs was a heresy with respect to their own traditions, which the pagans rejected precisely as being "fables of the ancients" (*al-awwalīn* = "the primordial ones"). Numerous passages in the Koran likewise point out that the Arabs believed neither in the immortality of the soul nor in resurrection, whereas their ancestors did believe in them.

[3] If in a certain respect a given Message addresses itself to given men, in another respect and in principle it addresses itself to man as such and, consequently and in a concrete manner, to a given individual situated outside the providential area of expansion of the Message, as destiny may determine. On the one hand: "They that are whole need not a physician"; but on the other hand: "Go ye therefore, and teach all nations."

tive tribes, to say nothing of the absurd and appalling clash between the *conquistadores* and the Indians of Peru and Mexico. However, even within these contexts, which to say the least are problematical—in divergent ways—there are always cases where the authentic and legitimate confrontation repeats itself: there have always and everywhere been saints who preach and, in their wake, pagans who convert independently of any constraint.[4] Be that as it may, our intention is to speak of divine Messages, not of human amalgams which veil the reason for their existence.

If nascent Islam had to deal with a massive paganism, such was not the case with Christianity, which at its beginning was confronted with a religion valid in itself, but nonetheless decadent in more than one respect.[5] In every religion there are two domains: firstly that which must be, and which consequently cannot not be; secondly that which may or may not be, and which therefore does not necessarily have to be; heresy is that which cannot be and which therefore is incompatible with the essential intention of the religion. The first domain is that of dogma; the second is that of interpretation and elaboration. Mosaic law clearly pertains to that which must be; however a great number of rabbinical speculations, interpretations, and regulations pertain no less clearly to that which may or may not be, hence to that which could be otherwise; which is to say, to that which, while remaining formally on the plane of orthodoxy, is determined by human tendencies, whether legitimately or abusively.[6] Thus in principle, there are two orthodoxies, one that is impeccable and one that is problematical,

[4] It is known that most of the American Indians were Christianized by force; even so, an Indian who respected the ancient religion told us that the Sermon on the Mount is the most beautiful discourse there is. Many Indians find no objection in practicing both religions: the old one because it seems obvious to them, and the new one because of the irresistible character of Christ.

[5] See the chapter, "La Marge humaine", in our book *Forme et Substance dans les Religions*.

[6] Which led Jesus to speak of "human prescriptions" even though they were "traditional".

or more precisely one that is evident or at least highly plausible and another born of the concern to "dot one's i's" and to "split hairs".

Now Christ takes to task *a priori* the moral mentality of the Pharisees,[7] then their problematic interpretations of the Law, but he also abolishes, *a posteriori* and by way of consequence, the Law itself; or rather, he intends to give the Law a new and more interiorized form, more demanding although less burdensome, by means of the Sacraments; therefore in his intention there is renewal and not abolition. In the case of the Pharisaic prescriptions, Christ acts as Doctor of the Law; in the case of Mosaic orthodoxy, he acts on the contrary as law-giving Prophet; he is thus independent of a given orthodoxy or a given "form", but not of orthodoxy as such, namely not of the "spirit".

A very grave factor in the Judaism of that epoch was the doctrinal schism between Pharisees and Sadducees, or rather the element of heterodoxy which created this situation. The Pharisees adhered to interpreting the *Torah* according to a casuistry pushed to extremes, and in a manner that favored formalism and outwardness, and in some respects even facileness; but at the same time they had the merit of rendering the religion meaningful to the people. The Sadducees on the contrary, culled largely from among the priests and the aristocrats, adhered above all to the cult of the Temple and opposed the exegesis of the Pharisees, which in their opinion was too free and too complex, while themselves professing grave heresies on the subject of eschatology. The fact that they rejected the hermeneutical oral Tradition—the *Mishnah*[8]—and that they denied the immortality of the soul,[9] the resurrection of the body, and the existence of angels—this

---

[7] Even from the point of view of the most orthodox Judaism, no one has the possibility of affirming peremptorily that the "scribes and Pharisees" did not deserve the reproaches of Christ, whereas one is obliged to admit that their ancestors deserved the Babylonian captivity. The brahmins at the time of the Buddha were quite decadent, and the Hindus in principle have no difficulty in admitting it, without however feeling obliged to condemn the brahmanic caste or *a fortiori* Brahmanism.

[8] The *a priori* oral character of this Tradition did not preclude its being fixed in books later, any more than this fixation precludes its being transmitted orally.

[9] The negation of immortality finds no support, of course, in the *Torah*. Quite the contrary: "And Enoch walked with God, and was seen no more: because God took him" (Gen. 5:24). "And no man hath known of his sepulcher (of Moses) until this present day" (Deut. 34:6). "Samuel said to Saul: Why hast thou disquieted me, to bring me up?" (I Sam. 28:15). "As they went on, walking and talking together behold a fiery

fact takes on all the more gravity in that the Sadducees held authority in the Temple; now the contradictory combination of these two facts shows precisely that the situation of Judaism in the face of Christ was not that of a perfectly homogeneous and fully orthodox religion, and that the nascent Church was clearly aware of this, to say the least.

Pure and simple logic is one thing, scriptural and semantic, or possibly moralistic, logic is another; the first operates on the basis of realities and concepts, and the second on the basis of words, then of sentiments, and even of self-interest. The Jewish contemporaries of Christ appear to have known or practiced rather the second type of logic, which on its own is enough to explain the unfathomable inconsequence on the part of the Sadducees for following a religious Law without believing in the hereafter, and the no less extraordinary illogicality of the Pharisees in tolerating the Sadducees in the Temple.[10] Before accusing Jesus of the sin of heresy, the "doctors of the Law" would have done well to come to an agreement on their own ortho-doxy[11] and since they were not in agreement, it appears that, even from their own point of view, they had much to learn from Christ, and in this sense he remains, in principle, a Master within the very framework of Judaism.[12] Within this framework, moreover, there

chariot and fiery horses parted them both asunder: and Elias went up by a whirlwind into Heaven" (II Kings 2:11).

[10] Tolerating them for the simple reason that they too were faithful to the letter of the *Torah*, even while denying eschatology because the *Torah* does not speak of it, although the *Torah* presupposes it essentially on pain of being absurd. Besides, this silence or this ellipsism—rather relative in fact—of the *Torah* does not prevent the *Mishnah* from being explicit; and to reject the *Mishnah*—as the Sadducees did—is to reject the *Torah* as well.

[11] When Christ permits his disciples not to wash their hands before meals, he is mak-ing no innovation; he is in agreement with the Sadducees who reject this practice as having been invented by the Pharisees.

[12] If a Judaizing Christianity is possible, a Christianizing Judaism is equally possible: there are in fact practicing Jews who accept Jesus as a prophet of Israel, attributing the Christic doctrine to a *de facto* uncomprehended esoterism, and without forgetting that the invectives uttered by the Jewish Prophets prefigure those of Christ. "Woe unto them that decree unrighteous decrees, and that write grievousness which they have prescribed" (Is. 10:1). "For my people have committed two evils; they have forsaken me the fountain of living waters, and hewed them out cisterns, broken cisterns, that can hold no water" (Jer. 2:13). The fact that such sayings are addressed to the contem-poraries of the ancient Prophets does not in any way prevent them from also being

was a third group, the Essenes, who were most likely the ancestors of the Cabalists and who were remarkably close to the spirit of Jesus; but despite this they did not become Christians, which calls to mind, theoretically at least, the saying in the Gospel: "They that are whole need not a physician."

This context calls for a remark: to accuse the Jews of "deicide" is just as absurd as to claim that they cannot be blamed for the death of Jesus, since only a minority was responsible for it. On the one hand—leaving aside the fact that God could not be the victim of a homicide—the Jews obviously did not acknowledge that Jesus is God; on the other hand, what matters is not the question of knowing which individuals condemned Jesus, but the fact that the majority of Jews are traditionally in agreement that he was justly condemned, which from the Christian point of view constitutes a co-responsibility; not to mention the views of the *Talmud*, which one cannot ask the Christians to take lightly. We are the first to admit that Mosaism had the right to survive—the advent of Islam is, paradoxically, an indirect proof of this—but it is necessary to see the facts as they are, whatever conclusions one believes should be drawn from them. One thing is certain, and it is that one cannot be saved by the hatred of anyone; one is saved by the love of God, even if this love was to be accompanied by some outward injustice due to a pardonable lack of understanding—an injustice set aside and therefore non-determinative.

Subjectively, one can avoid committing oneself to a religious message for two reasons, one positive and one negative: one might not commit to it out of love for the truth—the truth in a given form—but again, one might refuse it out of a hatred of true spirituality, inwardness, and asceticism, hence out of a kind of worldliness; this was the case with a great number of the contemporaries of Jesus, who believed that they had established between God and themselves a *modus vivendi* well sheltered by formal rectitude, whereas in reality God likes to shatter and to renew forms or the husks of things; for He wants our hearts and is not content with our actions alone. It is upon this aspect that Christ strongly insisted; too strongly in the opinion of the "orthodox", but not too strongly from the point of view of the real needs of men.

applied in a particular way to the contemporaries of Christ, and in a general way to men of every epoch and origin.

Be that as it may, even if Europe had had no need of Christ, Israel would have needed Jesus. The Buddha rejected the *Veda*, yet the Brahmanists accepted him as an *Avatāra*; Christ did not reject the *Torah*, hence the Mosaists could all the more easily—or with less difficulty—have accepted him as a Prophet. In fact, Christianity seems to have done Judaism a service indirectly, just as Buddhism did for Brahmanism; not in the sense of a doctrinal influence of course, but in the sense that the new Revelation "catalyzed" the old ones and allowed them to become once again fully themselves, no doubt with some additional emphases.

As with Judaism and as with every religion, Christianity comprises a domain of things which may or may not be; in Saint Paul we see the first signs of this, which later became clearer with the Fathers, the councils, and the great theologians. The schism between the Catholic and the Orthodox Churches demonstrates moreover, if one acknowledges the legitimacy of each of these denominational positions, that what is in question here is the domain of the possible and not of the necessary.

Saint Paul inaugurated the "de-Judaization" of Christianity;[13] now one could conceive of a Christianity faithful at least to the fundamental prescriptions of Moses, and this Christianity has existed in fact. Certainly the "Europeanization" of Christianity was providential in a positive sense—which is indicated by the role of the Holy Spirit promised by Christ—but it was providential only in view of the extra-Judaic radiation of the new religion;[14] in principle Christianity could have remained a Jewish, hence "Judaized" esoterism. However: to say that the Christian message was destined to become a religion is to say that it had to become independent of the religion that constituted its original milieu; thus necessity plays in this case a much larger role than mere possibility. One

---

[13] The excessively unilateral interpretation of the "Old Law", as well as the misinterpretation of sexuality, derive from the Epistles and not from the Gospel. It was a question of bringing about the triumph on the one hand of a perspective of *bhakti*, and on the other hand of a morality more penitential than social, and more idealistic than realistic.

[14] This is to say that the intervention of the Paraclete would not have been necessary had Providence not foreseen the primarily occidental expansion of Christianity.

cannot say as much of later theological and legal "crystallizations"; for if the apostolic epoch benefited from the inspiration of the Holy Spirit to an "eminent degree", the following epochs pertain more and more to the "human margin": the assistance of the Holy Spirit is not absent, for it is guaranteed, but it is indirect and largely takes account of human "temperaments", on the basis of what is acquired and immutable.

With the problem of the papacy for example, we are in the domain of what we could call a "relative orthodoxy", which concedes to man the right to "points of view", hence to options relatively justified but nonetheless replaceable in principle. No doubt, the papacy is necessary or inevitable in the Latin and Latinized world; but the fact remains that the quality of prophet and emperor which the pope attributes to himself in practice, is at the very least a two-edged sword; thus the Greeks were not mistaken in deeming these two functions to be ill-suited to the vicar of Saint Peter, and history fully corroborates their view.[15]

We have pointed out above, that in the case of the pagan Arabs, their reasons for resisting the new Message were of a profane and passional order, not of a spiritual order. In the case of the ancient Europeans, who are also classified as "pagans"—though with far less justification—their reasons for refusal were partly positive and partly negative: positive to the extent that they were founded on traditional and intellectual values—which could not have been the case with the ancient Arabs[16]—and negative to the extent that, on the

---

[15] For the Greeks, the words of Christ to Peter near the Lake of Tiberias have primarily the meaning of a "rehabilitation" after the three denials, which appears moreover to follow from the divine Master's three previous questions; it is also permissible to think that this rehabilitation at the same time effaced the shadow left by the *retro Satanas* which Christ hurled at Peter on the threshold of the Passion. No one contests the fact that Peter enjoyed a certain pre-eminence; nonetheless, the "beloved disciple" and adopted son of Mary was John, and the great organizer of the nascent Church was Paul, which indicates that this pre-eminence of Peter had nothing absolute about it; it cannot in any case justify the abuses of the papacy, the major consequences of which are the Renaissance, the Lutheran reaction, and in our times the seizing of the Church by the modernists.

[16] Except for the "pure" (*hanīf, hunafāʾ*), who had preserved intact the monotheism of

contrary, they resulted from the worship of the here-below, hence from worldliness in all its forms. The resistance of the philosophers to Christianity was negative when their point of view was rationalist, profane, and worldly, but it was positive when the point of view was truly sapiential—the two points of view often being curiously mingled due to the ambiguity of the ambience.[17] If we may have recourse in this context to the Hindu notions of *bhakti* and *jnāna*, we would say that in the clash between nascent Christianity and the Greco-Roman world, a *bhakti* in the full force of its vitality encountered a *jnāna* in full decadence; generally speaking, at least, and leaving out the initiatic mysteries as well as Neoplatonism.

As for Aristotelianism, we can confine ourselves here to the following consideration: on the one hand the Stagirite teaches the art of thinking correctly, but on the other hand he also induces one to think too much, to the detriment of intuition. Assuredly, syllogisms can be useful, but on the express condition that they be necessary; in other words, so long as syllogistic thinking is not superimposed as a systematic luxury upon a cognitive capacity it smothers while at the same time implicitly seeming to postulate the impossibility of this very capacity. It is as if, through groping continually, one no longer knew how to see, or as if the possession of an art compelled even its abusive use; or again, as if thought were there for logic, rather than logic for thought.

Nonetheless the Semites and the Semiticized peoples, who are voluntarists by vocation or by formation—that is, who are impulsive types more prone to inspiration from above than to intellection *ab intra*—had need of the Greeks to learn if not how to think, at least how to express themselves and sometimes even how to reason. The Semitic writer readily lets himself be carried away by his subject to the point of losing sight of the basic homogeneity of the subject matter being treated as well as of the homogeneity of its treatment, all the more so in that he thinks largely by associations of ideas and by discontinuous intuitions; now the guarantee for inspirations is often the correct character of thought—or let us say simply of logic—owing to the principle of

Abraham and Ishmael; they accepted Islam without resistance. As for Arab polytheism, one must not lose sight of the fact that it had no traditional basis, and that on the contrary it was nothing but a syncretism of borrowed divinities, and that certain idols even had an altogether historical and empirical origin.

[17] The ambiguity of Stoicism is characteristic in this respect.

affinities and on condition, of course, that logic have access to sufficient information and that it go hand in hand with the gift of intellection.

In the opinion of all unbelievers, it is the absurdities contained in the sacred Scriptures which above all stand in the way of the credibility of the Message; although we have more than once had occasion to speak of this error arising from an ignorant and hasty reading, we cannot refrain from returning to it again in this context. First of all, it is necessary to consider a Scripture in its totality and not be hypnotized, with perfect myopia, by a fragmentary difficulty, which after all is the perspective of the devil, who disparages a mountain because of a fissure and, inversely, praises an evil because of an inevitable particle of good. When Scripture is considered in its totality it imparts its overall value and supernatural character to whomever is not blinded by any prejudice and who has been able to preserve intact the normally human sensibility for the majestic and the sacred. No doubt, the majesty of the Biblical or Vedic style can be imitated, and profane literature offers us a few more or less successful examples of this; but what cannot be imitated is the depth of the meanings and the theurgic radiation of divinely inspired Texts.

Then, in order to judge Scriptural passages that are at first sight problematical, one would have to become acquainted with the traditional commentaries; for the *Torah* it is the rabbinical and cabalistic interpretations that resolve its material as well as moral enigmas. In many cases however, it is not necessary to have recourse to the insights of the commentators, since the real meaning is so obviously in the nature of things; for example in the story of Jacob and Esau, it suffices to know certain laws concerning the play of *Māyā* to be able to eliminate the stumbling-block. The unadvised reader finds it strange, to say the least, that Jacob, at the instigation of Rebecca but also of his own will, deceives Isaac his father by posing as Esau; in reality there was no immoral initiative but a conflict of planes: a particular divine Will ran counter to a social situation. For even though Esau was the eldest, he was visibly unworthy of his birthright, which he sold unbeknownst to his father; if there was deceit, it was above all here. In saying, "I am Esau", Jacob meant, "I am what Esau ought to be, but could not and would not be"; hence, "I am the true Esau". If there is a fault it is also on the part of Isaac, who had a near blind preference for his elder son despite the disqualification of the latter;[18] in the end, Isaac recognized Jacob's priority, Jacob and Esau were reconciled, and God sanctioned the situation, which proves that Jacob and his mother were right.[19] In the opinion of the rabbis, Jacob nevertheless had to expiate the appearance of fraud in all that he had to suffer later on, above all from his own sons; in this, his case is similar to that of Solomon, who also had to expiate apparent faults while being irreproachable, esoterically speaking.[20]

In reading in Genesis that "Cain knew his wife", many "critical minds" have wondered where she came from, since the only existing woman in that epoch was Eve; and they have concluded, hastily to say the least and untroubled by any sense of proportion whatsoever, that the Bible is not worth taking seriously nor, in consequence, is religion. In reality it is a question here of an ellipsis, frequent in sacred Scriptures; in most cases it is either the oral tradition or the inspired commentary, or again a foreign but parallel tradition, that provides the key to the enigma. In the case of Cain's wife it is the Arab tradition that resolves the difficulty, and it is moreover possible that this difficulty coincides with some Jewish tradition: Cain and Abel were each born with a twin sister; Abel was stronger and more virtuous than Cain, but Cain's sister was more beautiful than Abel's. Now for this reason Cain desired to marry his own twin sister, but since the principle of blood

---

[18] This preference could have been motivated either by a particular quality of Esau—precious in the eyes of Isaac for reasons of complementarity—or simply by the law of primogeniture, sacred to the ancient Semites; in this latter case, the attitude of Isaac would be analogous to that of Abu Bakr's denying Fatimah the right to her inheritance, for legal reasons and contrary to certain rights of another order.

[19] Before blessing Jacob, Isaac said: "See, the smell of my son is as the smell of a field which the Lord hath blessed" (Gen. 27:27). According to the *Zohar*, the reference here is not to the smell of Esau's garment but to the perfume of the spiritual or paradisal garment of Jacob, and that is why Isaac blessed him; this perfume revealed the "true son", whatever might have been his name.

[20] The Bible, whose perspective is above all legalistic since it is moral, reproaches Solomon for having constructed temples for the divinities of his foreign wives, but it adds nonetheless that Solomon "slept with his fathers", a formula which is also used in speaking of David and which refers to posthumous Beatitude. It would be contradictory, to say the least, to doubt the salvation of an author whose writings are included in the Bible; if there are differences of opinion on the subject of Solomon, it is because of a conflict of levels and not because of an ambiguity situated on one and the same plane.

relations demands that the choice of a partner be the most distant one, Abel offered—in the name of God—his twin sister to Cain; Cain refused, and for that reason Abel conceived the idea of a trial by ordeal: if God would not accept Cain's offering, Cain would have to submit; what happened is well known. We will add that this story, far from being a clumsy fable, is, on the contrary, crystalline in its symbolism by reason of the geometry of compensatory relationships that it presents.

Another scriptural difficulty is the following, drawn from the Koran this time: "And We (*Allāh*) bestowed upon him (upon Abraham) Isaac and Jacob, and each of them We guided (*hadaynā = hudā*); and Noah did We guide aforetime; and of his seed (Abraham's): David and Solomon and Job and Joseph and Moses and Aaron; thus do We reward those who realize the good (*muhsinūn = ihsān*). And Zechariah and John (the Baptist) and Jesus and Elias, each one of them was among the poles of sanctity (*sālihūn = sulh*);[21] likewise, Ishmael and Elisha and Jonah and Lot; and to each of these We have bestowed excellence above the entire world (*faddalnā = fadl*)" (*Sūrah* "Cattle" [6]:84-86). The unforewarned reader will undoubtedly be shocked by the seemingly anachronistic enumeration and also of the tautological platitude; now it is important to know that the laudatory expressions have here a particular function of classification; and as for the apparent anachronisms it is a question in this text, precisely, of typological categories and not of chronology. The common notions of "guidance" (*hudā*),[22] "right action" (*ihsān*),[23] "piety" (*sulh*), and "favor" (*fadl*)[24]

---

[21] The literal meaning is "reconciling and appeasing piety", but since it is a question of Prophets we have permitted ourselves to comment while translating, for it goes without saying that in certain cases the quality of the substantive determines the interpretation of the adjective. Besides, in more than one passage in the Koran the adjectives defining piety have as their function, not to convince us needlessly that the Prophets were pious, but on the contrary to lend the prestige of the Prophets to these notions.

[22] The meaning here is that of "primordial guidance", or at least "original" or "initial" guidance from the point of view of Semitic monotheism.

[23] *Ihsān* comprises the subjective meaning of "sincerity"—to act as if we were seeing God, He who sees us—and the objective meaning of "action productive of good"; with David and Solomon this good is the founding of Jewish royalty and the construction of the temple. If these two kings were named before personages who preceded them it is perhaps because of their mystical and esoteric eminence, manifested by the Psalms and the Song of Songs.

[24] The term "favor" here takes on the particular meaning of "success" or "glory" after

assume in this context special significations that cancel any aspect of pleonasm about them, but which we have no need to explain further in connection with these personages;[25] it suffices to illustrate, with the aid of this Koranic example, the general point that scriptural expressions appearing unimportant, even absurd, conceal a precise and plausible meaning.

But such subtleties of expression are a small matter compared with the dogmatic ellipsisms contained in sacred Scriptures. *Credibile quia ineptum est*,[26] as Tertullian said; in other words, the apparent ineptness is often the measure of the supernatural; or it is the measure of the ellipsism of the expression, hence of the superabundance of implicit and partly inexpressible meanings. Let us mention by way of example the eternity of an afterlife either blissful or woeful: firstly the idea that something which has a beginning could have no end, and then the idea that a limited cause could have an unlimited consequence. Both conceptions are ellipses, and we could point out and explain the links that have been left unmentioned—we have done this on other occasions—but what is important here is to point out that these ideas suggest, in an adequate and efficacious manner, man's position between contingency and the Absolute; and also to recall that eschatological dogmas are directed to moral and existential intuition rather than to reason or common sense.

But apparent absurdity is found not only in a given religious text, but also and even above all in the dogmatic contradictions separating religions. Certainly, God cannot contradict Himself in essence, but He can appear to contradict Himself within forms and levels; the phenomenon of multiple subjectivity is contradictory, but subjectivity

providential tribulations.

[25] It should be borne in mind that the Koran presupposes not only the Biblical texts but also the Arab and Talmudic traditions; and sometimes these traditions more so than the Bible.

[26] Later rendered as: *Credo quia absurdum.* Quite curiously, the Shinto commentator Motoori Norinaga has expressed himself in a similar manner: "Who would have invented such a ridiculous and unbelievable story if it were not true?"

in itself cannot be so, and the same holds true for certain scriptural passages or for the religions themselves. The plurality of religions is no more contradictory than the plurality of individuals: in Revelation, God as it were makes Himself an individual in order to address the individual; the homogeneity with respect to other Revelations is inward and not outward. If humanity were not diverse, a single divine individualization would suffice; but man is diverse not only from the point of view of ethnic temperaments, but also from that of spiritual possibilities; the diverse combinations of these two things make possible and necessary the diversity of Revelations.

What is "historical fact" for Christianity in particular and the Bible in general, becomes "symbol" in Islam, at least to a great extent if not always; the fundamental Message of Islam uses Christian facts like stones for a new building, the function of the stones being modified according to their new use. It cannot be emphasized enough that in every religion there are elements which are to be taken literally and others which are symbolic and which have through their new interpretation—evidently slanted but intrinsically valid—a didactic and regulating function for the souls of the faithful. All told, the principial and archetypal Model of "myth"—or of "religious imagery"—is invariable: it is the Logos who shines in the darkness; who at first is uncomprehended and who then triumphs; who is uncomprehended because darkness is darkness, and who triumphs because Light is Light. And it is always the Logos, from the moment his trajectory enters the realm of human diversity, who gives rise by polarization to the diverse religious systems; in which case, the human diversity is combined with the divine Infinitude, hence with inexhaustible Possibility.

In this order of ideas, the question may arise of knowing to what extent a believer has the right or the duty to recognize the spiritual worth or even the full validity of other religions. In principle and *a priori*, no such obligation could exist, for each religion possesses within itself everything man needs; but in fact and in the context of unavoidable experiences, this question is finally bound to arise. Leaving aside intuition on the one hand, and the imponderables of grace on the other, the first argument in favor of the validity of foreign religions is the irrefutable character of their intrinsic content: every religion has its axioms that, from its vantage point, are metaphysically, spiritually, and humanly evident. To understand the religious phenomenon is to understand this quasi-ontological autonomy; no doubt, it can be attacked from without, but this could not weaken the internal logic of the religious system, nor the graces which corroborate that logic or that sacramental symbolism.

The proof that "our" religion is not the only true one is provided, not only by what we can grasp of the intrinsic truth of other religions, but also by the simple fact of their presence and their power;[27] how can it be explained that God, if He wished to save the world by means of a single religion, should have permitted the existence of so many other religions which bar its way, and which do so all the more effectively and irrevocably, precisely, because they comprise in substance the same contents as the religion considered as "ours"?

It is a fact of common experience that men, even when becoming acquainted with foreign doctrines, or especially when so doing, consider it perfectly logical to reason in terms of the doctrine in which they have grown up; one finds it altogether natural for French believers to reason ingeniously in terms of Catholicism, and to find it logically irresistible, whereas Greek or Russian believers do the same in terms of Orthodoxy; and each of them no less than the others reason in terms of their hereditary conviction even while being perfectly well aware of the positions of those whom they consider to be heretics— positions that are usually if not always just as plausible as theirs. Human subjectivity, even on the plane of logic, identifies itself with the ideological ambience in which it was formed; whence the quasi-innate prejudices that determine for good or ill religious reasonings, and whence also a lack of imagination, excusable or inexcusable as the case may be, in short a deep-seated incapacity to put oneself in the place of subjectivities rooted in other ambiences.[28] All of this is based,

---

[27] It is to this aspect that the argument of Gamaliel refers: if this argument, accorded so much importance by Christians, is not false, then it also applies to Islam, which came forth out of nothing and imposed itself in a miraculously short time on a vast portion of the world. This argument, however, cannot be used in favor of the modern errors which, precisely, are not religions, and which have no need of any celestial aid to "have the wind in their sails".

[28] One cannot reproach a Massignon with this, whose conciliatory thesis on the subject of Islam would be perfectly usable in the framework of Christian theology, at least as an optional interpretation. Outside the Semitic world, we see more than one case of "rehabilitation"—or of integration—of foreign elements by a given traditional world: Hinduism cannot fully accept the Buddha without ruining itself, but it takes note of the fact that the Buddha was one of the great *Avatāra*s and accords him the venera-

of course, on the exclusivism of religion; men have no eschatological interest—or believe they have none—in challenging this exclusivism, quite the contrary. Nonetheless, this "instinct of self-preservation" has nothing to do with pure intelligence nor with the total truth; and it remains to be seen on what chord of our spirit we place the accent, or upon what chord God wishes to place it.[29]

The basis for the "logical subjectivism" of believers lies in what may be termed "religious solipsism"; and this is unavoidable for two major reasons. Firstly, every religious Message is a Message of the Absolute; this character of Absoluteness penetrates the entire Message and confers upon it its quality of uniqueness. God speaks for the Inward and is not preoccupied with the outward as such; He proclaims "the Religion" in a form adapted to given human possibilities; He does not engage in "comparative religion". Secondly, the average man is not disposed to grasp this character of Absoluteness if it is not suggested to him by the uniqueness of its expression; and God has no intention of compromising this understanding with specifications stressing what is outward and relative, thus foreign to that which is the reason for the existence of the Message. But this could in no way bind esoterism: on the one hand because esoterism is not a religious Message and derives from the Intellect rather than from Revelation, and on the other hand because it is addressed to men who have no need of a suggestion of uniqueness and exclusivity, at the level of formulation, in order to grasp the character of Absoluteness in sacred enunciations.

All of this should serve to make it clear that we are as far as can be from approving a gratuitous and sentimentalist "ecumenism",

---

tion due to one of his rank, even while presenting awkward explanations concerning his role. In a manner at once analogous and different, the Shinto divinities became *Bodhisattvas*, sometimes through their own intervention, in dreams or visions or by way of oracles.

[29] Let us not forget that theology comprises necessarily, or nearly so, elements of universality: even while being obliged to affirm that there is "no salvation outside the Church", it admits nonetheless that Christ can save whom he will, and that there are everywhere souls which belong "invisibly" to the one and only Church. The Muslims—not to mention other Orientals—have similar reasonings, *mutatis mutandis.*

which does not distinguish between truth and error and which results in religious indifference and the cult of man. In reality what has to be understood is that the undeniable presence of transcendent truth, of the sacred, and of the supernatural—in forms other than that of our religion of birth—ought to lead us, not in the least to doubt the Absolute character proper to our religion, but simply to acknowledge the inherence of the Absolute in other doctrinal and sacramental symbols which manifest and communicate it by definition, but which also by definition are relative and limited—since they belong to the formal order—despite their quality of uniqueness. This latter quality is necessary, as we have said, inasmuch as it testifies to the Absolute, but is merely indicative from the point of view of the Absolute in itself, which manifests itself necessarily by uniqueness, yet just as necessarily—by virtue of its Infinitude—by the diversity of forms.

All of these considerations raise the following questions, which we have already answered in one way or another: how can a man, who observes that his religion of birth or adoption is visibly incapable of saving the whole of humanity, still believe that it is the only saving religion? And how can a man, who moreover observes the existence of other religions, powerfully established and having the same claim, persist in believing that God, sincerely desirous of saving the world, should have found no other means of doing so than by instituting one sole religion, strongly colored by particular ethnic and historical features—as it must necessarily be—and doomed in advance to failure as regards the goal in question? Finally, why is it that in the vast majority of cases the adherent of a given religion or denomination remains unmoved by the arguments of another given religion or denomination, even when he has studied it as much as it can be studied?

Doubtless, these questions do not arise *a priori*, but in the end they arise after centuries of experience, although any quantitative evaluation would perforce have to be relative. And the fact that these questions arise and that they compromise to a great extent religion as such which, clearly, has no adequate means of answering them, shows that they arise legitimately and providentially, and that in the religions there is, to the very extent of their exclusivism, an aspect of insufficiency, normal no doubt but nonetheless detrimental in the final analysis.

The divine origin and the majesty of the religions implies that they must contain all truth and all answers; and there, precisely, lies the mystery and the role of esoterism. When the religious phenomenon, hard-pressed as it were by a badly interpreted experience, appears to be at the end of its resources, esoterism springs forth from the very depths of this phenomenon to show that Heaven cannot contradict itself; that a given religion in reality sums up all religions and that all religion is to be found in a given religion, because Truth is one. In other words: the contrast between the absolute character of Revelation and its aspect of relativity constitutes indirectly one more proof—along with the direct and historical proofs—both of the reality and the necessity of the esoteric dimension proper to all religion; so much so that the religions, at the very moment when they seem to be defeated by experience, affirm themselves victoriously on every level owing to their very essence.

Religious divergences make us think of the contradictions between the visions of the mystics, even though there is no common measure between the two, except that in both cases there is an intrinsic underlying truth: one mystic paints a rather despairing picture of purgatory, while another insists on a joy of hope which reigns there, each perspective being supported by imagery that portrays it concretely; the symbolism is combined with an isolating fragmentariness and a one-sided sentimentalism. As in the case of the religions, the formal contradictions of mystical imagery do not invalidate the integral truth, whose aspects they accentuate in terms of a particular perspective of fear or love; but we do not need to have recourse to esoterism here to bring out the truth; theology provides it in distinguishing at the outset between the contents of belief, according to whether they are necessary, recommended, or simply possible.

Christianity is founded upon the unique Incarnation and the unique Redemption; and then, by way of consequence and quasi-exclusively, upon sacrifice and sacramental life. That is, it is founded upon the uniqueness of Christ and his gifts, and upon the sacrificial character of his personality and his life; these elements, together with the sacrificial and sacramental piety that they require, are considered to be the sole conditions and guarantees of salvation, although it is admitted that they may act exceptionally within the framework of another religion in an underlying fashion.

Islam for its part intends to be founded upon the Truth that has always been and the Faith that has always been: on the one hand it is based upon the immutable Reality of God—Unity, Omniscience, Omnipotence, Mercy—and on the invariability of His ways, and on the other hand upon the inalienable constants of the theomorphic nature of man; by way of consequence, man's attitude will be obedience: either it is an obedience conforming with this nature, or it will be sacrificial. The Truth of God and the quality of Faith, together with the obediential piety and the operative sincerity that they require, are considered to be the sole conditions and guarantees of salvation, although it is admitted that they may act exceptionally within the framework of another religion in an underlying fashion.

It is from these differences of perspective that inevitable divergences of application result and thereby also the dissonances in certain symbolisms, to the very extent that they are contingent.

—— ·:· ——

Here we could insert a consideration—although its substance is known to our regular readers—which is quite particular but characteristic of interdenominational misunderstandings: according to a common idea, all the more tenacious in that its content is materially and psychologically impossible, Muslim asceticism would be Christian, even Buddhist, in origin, as if the ambiguity of earthly pleasures could be overlooked by a perspective as concerned with the nature of things as Islam is. The apparent contradiction in the moral comportment of Muslims is not in their philosophy, it is in things themselves; if Islam on the one hand recognizes the positive quality of sexuality, on the other hand it is aware of the danger involved in pleasure as such, the two points of view coexisting and interweaving in practice as well as in theory. On the one hand, the Sufi turns away from earthly beauty, as if he were saying: "Since this is not God, it is not beauty; God alone possesses it." Yet on the other hand he contemplates and accepts beauty: "Since this is beauty and nothing else, it can only be that of God, even here." Everything lies in balancing both attitudes: to accept beauty or any other value "in the Name of God" and without excess, and conjointly with certain refusals that reinforce the right to this acceptance. The classical definition of the good as being situated between two contrary excesses, finds here its full meaning, in the sense that added to this wisely acquired good there is a vertical dimension, that of Heaven which blesses and attracts, or which sanctifies and reintegrates. Assuredly, earthly gardens can cause us to forget the celestial Garden and to "let go of the prey for its shadow"; but in reality—and it is here that contemplative "recollection" neutralizes seduction and outwardness—the earthly garden is Paradise veiled.

To believe only what one "sees": this prejudice, as crude as it is common, leads us to insert a comment here. Wanting to believe only what they see, scientists condemn themselves to seeing only what they believe; for them the question of logic comes down to their desire not to see what they do not want to believe. Scientism in fact is less interested in the real as such—which necessarily goes beyond our limitations—than in what is non-contradictory, therefore in what is logical, or more precisely, in what is empirically logical; thus in what is logical *de facto* according to a given experience, and not in what is logical *de jure* in accordance with the nature of things. In reality the "planimetric" recording of perceptions and the elimination of the apparently contradictory are too often only the measure of a specific type of ignorance, even of a specific type of stupidity; the pedants of "exact science" are moreover incapable of evaluating what is implied by the existential paradoxes in which we live, beginning with the phenomenon of subjectivity, which is contradictory in practice. Subjectivity is intrinsically unique while being extrinsically multiple; now if the spectacle of a plurality of subjectivities other than our own causes us no great perplexity, how can one explain "scientifically"—namely, avoiding or eliminating all contradiction—that "I alone" am "I"? So-called "exact" science can find no reason whatsoever for this apparent absurdity, any more than it can for that other logical and empirical contradiction which is the limitlessness of space, time, and the other existential categories. Whether we like it or not, we live surrounded by mysteries, that logically and existentially draw us towards transcendence.

Even if "expertly learned men" could observe the non-contradiction of all possible objective phenomena, there still would remain the contradictory enigma of the scission between the objective universe and the observing subject, not to mention the "scientifically" insoluble problem of that flagrant contradiction which is the empirical uniqueness of a particular subject, namely the problem we have just alluded to; and even if we limit ourselves to the objective world, of which precisely the limitlessness constitutes a contradiction since it is inconceivable according to empirical logic, how can we believe for an instant that the day will finally come when we can fit it into a homogeneous and exhaustive system? And how can we fail to see the fundamental and inevitable contradiction between scientistic logic—which is moreover intrinsically deficient since it lacks sufficient data—and the infinity as well as the complexity of the real, which scientism sets itself out to explore, to exhaust, and to label and classify? The fundamental contradiction of scientism is to want to explain the real without the help of that initial science which is metaphysics, hence not to know that only the science of the Absolute gives meaning and discipline to the science of the relative; and not to know at the same stroke that the science of the relative, when it is deprived of this assistance, can only lead to suicide, beginning with that of the intelligence, then with that of the human, and in the end with that of humanity. The absurdity of scientism is the contradiction between the finite and the Infinite, that is, the impossibility of reducing the latter to the former, and the incapacity to integrate the former into the latter; and also the inability to understand that an erudition which cuts itself off from initial Unity can lead only to the innumerable, hence to the indefinite, to shattering, and to nothingness.

If therefore the scientific method, or the conceptual system (*die Weltanschauung*) resulting from it, intends to have the privilege of excluding contradictions, it goes without saying that it accuses methods or systems, which in its opinion are extra-scientific, with the defect of accepting what is contradictory; as if there could exist a human and traditional thought which accepts the contradictory *de jure* and not only *de facto*, and as if what is contradictory in religion— supposing that it is not merely in the minds of the scientists—did not imply the consciousness of an underlying non-contradiction, known by God alone! What is the significance of the theological opinion that the human mind has limits, and what is the meaning of the mysteries, inasmuch as they are supposed to transcend reason, if not that man is incapable of perceiving the total and homogeneous reality behind the contradictions at which his shortsightedness stops? Recourse to the Divine authority of Revelation means nothing other than that, and this is so obvious that one would like to excuse oneself for pointing it out.

The man who wishes to know the visible—to know it both in its entirety and depth—is obliged for that very reason to know the Invisible, on pain of absurdity and ineffectualness; to know it according to the principles which the very nature of the Invisible imposes on the human mind; hence to know it by being aware that the solution to the contradictions of the objective world is found only in the transpersonal essence of the subject, namely in the pure Intellect.

Besides—and this is another question altogether—how can the adepts of a scientism which sets out to reduce total Reality to a clockwork mechanism, fail to see that the absurd—not merely in the guise of the unknown in this case, but as a manifestation of the indefinite and thereby of the unintelligible as such—is an integral part of the shimmering of *Māyā*, and thereby of the economy of the Universe? One of the most difficult things, morally, is to concede the metaphysical right of existence to what is existentially absurd, to do so not in theory alone, but upon concrete contact with absurdity; to be able to do so amounts almost to the victory over the dragon. Now before wishing to abolish the absurd that is merely apparent, it is necessary to acknowledge the ineluctable presence of the absurd as such, that cannot possibly be reabsorbed into the intelligible save in its function as a necessary element in the equilibrium of things. For Reality does not restrict itself to revealing its aspects of geometry, it also likes to conceal itself and to play hide-and-seek; hence it would be surprising if it consented to unveil itself totally to mathematical minds; were it to consent to this it would not be *Māyā*. Man is contingent and he is condemned to contingency, and contingency implies by definition the insoluble and the absurd.

Everything here is a question of causality: there are phenomena which seem absurd to us so long as we are unaware of their causes, or because we are unaware of these; and there are other phenomena which are absurd in themselves and which have no other cause than the cosmic necessity for that which has no necessity. Likewise there are possibilities which have no function other than to manifest the impossible, to the very extent that this can still be possible; and this is possible at least in a symbolic way, yet sufficiently clear to manifest the intention of impossibility or absurdity.

—— ∴ ——

A proof often advanced in favor of religion, but rarely understood to its full extent, is the argument of the moral efficacy of divine Legislation: indeed what becomes of human society when deprived of a Law founded upon the authority of God? Unbelievers, who as a general rule have but a highly limited and partly false idea of human nature—otherwise they would not be unbelievers—will answer that it suffices to replace the religious Law with a civil Law founded upon the common interest; now the opinion of the "free thinkers" concerning the public good depends upon their scale of values, hence upon their idea of man and thereby of the meaning of life. But what has been instituted by an individual can always be abolished by another individual; philosophies change with tastes, they follow the downward slope of history, because as soon as man is separated from his reason for existence rooted in God, he can only slide downwards, according to the law of gravity which applies to the human order as well as to the physical order, notwithstanding the periodic renewal effected by the religions, the sages, and the saints.[30]

Now the fact that the divine Law, inasmuch as it is fundamental and thereby universal,[31] is finally the only efficacious one—to the degree that a Law can and must be so—this fact shows that it is a Message of Truth; it alone is incontestable and irreplaceable. Certainly, the contemporary world still possesses codes and civil laws; however, even then, for the general mentality there is less and less an authority

---

[30] The dreamers of the eighteenth century, unaware of being hereditarily influenced by Christianity and imbued with ancient civism and freemasonic idealism, imagined that man is reasonable and that human reason coincides with their ideology; but this ideology is, to say the least, fragmentary and rendered inoperative in advance by the subversive cult of man. What they did not foresee is that once man is separated from divine Authority, he does not in any way feel obliged to submit to human authority; as soon as he knows himself to be independent of all authority other than his own, nothing prevents him from inventing morals that reflect his errors and his vices and that are adorned in their turn with a veil of rationality, at least insofar as euphemisms still seem useful to him.

[31] There are revealed prescriptions which have in view not the nature of man—as does the Decalogue, notably—but particular conditions or circumstances.

which is such "by right", and not merely "in fact".[32] Moreover, the Law is made to protect not only society, but also the individual who is criminally prone; if on the one hand the "secular arm" inspires fear to the degree that badly intentioned men feel threatened by it, on the other hand these same men have no intrinsic motive to check their inclinations save for the fear of God. The threat of human justice is uncertain, hence relative; that of the divine Justice is absolute; for strictly speaking it is possible to escape men, but certainly not God.

In summary: an indirect proof of God is that without Divinity there is no authority, and without authority there is no efficacy; this is to say that the religious Message is indispensable—apart from its other imperatives—because without it no moral and social life is possible, except for a brief period that still lives off the residues of a disavowed heritage, although without admitting it. And this brings us to another extrinsic proof *a contrario* of God, although it is fundamentally the same: it is a fact of experience that common man on the whole, who is not disciplined out of any social necessity, and who, precisely, is only disciplined by religion and piety, degenerates in his behavior when he no longer has religion containing and penetrating him; and experience proves that the disappearance of faith and of morals brings about that of personal dignity and of private life, which in fact have meaning and value only if man possesses an immortal soul. It is hardly necessary to recall here that believing peasants and artisans are often of an aristocratic nature, and that they are so owing to religion; without forgetting that aristocracy in itself, namely nobility of sentiment and comportment along with the tendency to control and transcend oneself, derives from spirituality and draws its principles from it, consciously or unconsciously.

What the people need in order to find meaning in life, hence the possibility of earthly happiness, is religion and the crafts: religion because every man has need of it, and the crafts because they allow man to manifest his personality and to realize his vocation in the framework of a sapiential symbolism; every man loves intelligible

[32] For this same mentality, morality is something merely subjective, and, in consequence, transgression is an entirely relative thing; now a judiciary apparatus is rendered all but impotent in a society which no longer believes that a crime is a crime, and which in this way contributes to the psychoanalyzation of justice and the abolition of public security.

work and work well done.[33] Now industrialism has robbed the people of both things: on the one hand of religion, denied by scientism from which industry derives, and rendered implausible by the inhuman character of the ambience of machinery; and on the other hand of the crafts, replaced precisely by machines; so much so, that in spite of all the "social doctrines" of the Church and the nationalistic bourgeoisie, there is nothing left for the people to give meaning to their life and make them happy. The classic contradiction of traditional Catholicism is to want to maintain social hierarchy, and it is theoretically correct in wanting to do so, while accepting wholeheartedly—as an acquisition of "Christian civilization" which in fact has long been abolished—the scientism and the machinism that in fact compromise this hierarchy by cutting the people off, in practice, from humankind. The reverse error is based on the same cult of technology, with the difference that it is detrimental to the bourgeoisie rather than to the common people, in that it aims at reducing the entire society to a mechanistic inhumanity while on the other hand presenting it with an "opium" made of bitterness and frigidity which kills the very organ of happiness; for to be happy it is necessary to be a child, happiness being made of gratitude and trust, humanly speaking. The machine is opposed to man, consequently it is also opposed to God; in a world where it has become a norm, it abolishes both the human and the divine. The logical solution to the problem would be the return—which in fact has become impossible without a divine intervention—to the crafts and at the same time to religion,[34] and thereby to an ambience which is not opposed to what gives meaning to life; an ambience which, by not falsifying our sense of

---

[33] Along with work, and the religion which sanctifies it, the people also have need of a wisdom; this is what Richelieu did not understand when he attacked the guilds.

[34] This is what a Gandhi tried to realize, heroically but without results other than that of a good example and all sorts of initiatives that remained partial and local. As for the Church, the objection will no doubt be raised that it could not compromise itself by opposing the "irreversible" phenomenon which is industrialism; we would reply first of all that the truth has precedence over any consideration of opportuneness or of "irreversibility", and then, that the Church could always have affirmed its doctrinal position, to all intents and purposes, without having to be unrealistic on the level of facts; it could moreover have opted, with perfect logic and in accord with its entire past, for the monarchist and traditional right-wing which upheld it by definition, without having to compromise itself, in the eyes of some, with the ambiguous "right-wing" born in the nineteenth century in the shadow of the machine.

the real, does not make implausible what is evident. One of the greatest successes of the devil was to create around man surroundings in which God and immortality seem no longer believable.[35]

There are attenuating circumstances for doubt when man finds himself torn between the bad examples given in the name of religion and his own instinct for the primordial religion—torn without having the sufficient discernment to put everything in its proper place. A workman once told us that he felt close to God in virgin nature and not in a church, and one of Tolstoy's characters said in a story: "Where are there baptismal fonts as great as the ocean?" There is here a sensibility both for the universality of truth and for the sacred character of nature, but this cannot make us lose sight of the fact that persistence in such simplifications, which easily turn into narcissism, has no excuse in the final analysis; for man is made to transcend himself, and he ought to have this impulse even as a plant turning towards the sun. One sensibility begets another, one should not stop halfway.

There is, in the man who by nature is a "believer" or who "belongs to the elect", a legacy of the lost Paradise, and this is the instinct for the transcendent and the sense of the sacred; it is on the one hand the disposition to believe in the miraculous, and on the other hand the need to venerate and to worship. Normally speaking, to this twofold predisposition a twofold detachment should be added: one with regard to the world and earthly life and another with regard to the ego, to its dreams and its pretensions. The problem of the credibility of the religious Messages can be resolved only by starting from these facts, which are normative because they result from man's deiformity.

"Abram believed in the Lord; and the Lord counted it to him for righteousness" (Gen. 15:6): that is, Abraham's faith here was a merit because its object was something humanly impossible; the same is true for Mary's faith at the time of the Annunciation. The unbeliever by nature is not inclined to consider possible what is contrary to nature and consequently to reason; not to reason in itself, but to reason inasmuch as it does not possess the information which would allow it to

---

[35] And this certainly is not, in spite of all illusions, "Christian civilization".

understand the laws of the supernatural. There are three possible attitudes or reactions with regard to the supernatural: refusal, acceptance, and perplexity; the classic image of the latter being the attitude of the Apostle Thomas. "Blessed are they that have not seen, and yet have believed" (John 20:29): those who, before seeing, are predisposed to believe.[36] The unbeliever, on earth, believes only what he sees; the believer, in Heaven, sees all that he believes.

We are always astonished by the fact that unbelievers and even certain believers are strangely insensitive to the direct language of the sacred Messages: that they do not perceive from the very first that the Psalms, the Gospel, the *Upanishads*, the *Bhagavad Gītā* could only come from Heaven, and that—from the point of view of credibility—the spiritual perfume of these Books requires no theological analysis, nor any historical research.[37] Personally, even if we were neither metaphysician nor esoterist, we would be a believer without the least difficulty; upon contact with the sacred in all its forms we would be convinced right from the start. We would believe in God and immortality because their evidence appears in the very form of the Message; all the more in that to learn what God is, is to recall what we are.

A point of view which is readily lost sight of—should it even come to mind—when defending those who refuse the celestial Messages, is the very appearance of the Messengers themselves; now, to paraphrase or to cite some well-known formulas: "he who has seen the Prophet has seen God"; "God became man in order that man might become God". One has to have a very hardened heart not to be able to see this upon contact with such beings; and it is above all this hardness of heart that is deserving of blame, far more so than ideological scruples.

---

[36] For the Koran, faith (*īmān*) consists in "believing in what is hidden (*yu'minūna bil-ghayb*)" (*Sūrah* "The Cow" [2]:2).

[37] How, in reading the life and writings of a Honen Shonin, could one doubt the validity of the Amidist tradition and the sanctity of this personage? A tradition and a faith that produce such fruits, with such generosity and for so many centuries, can only be supernatural.

The combination of sanctity and beauty which characterizes the Messengers of Heaven is transmitted so to speak from the human theophanies to the sacred art which perpetuates it: the essentially intelligent and profound beauty of this art testifies to the truth which inspires it; it could not in any case be reduced to a human invention as regards the essential of its message. Sacred art is Heaven descended to earth, rather than earth reaching towards Heaven.[38]

An argument akin to the one we have just presented is the following, and we have made note of it more than once: if men were stupid enough to believe for millennia in the divine, the supernatural, immortality—assuming these are illusions—it is impossible that one fine day they became intelligent enough to be aware of their errors; that they became intelligent without there being any explanation as to how they became so and without any decisive moral acquisition to corroborate this miracle. And similarly: if men like Christ believed in the supernatural, it is impossible that men like the Encyclopedists were right not to believe in it.

Skeptical rationalism and titanic naturalism are the two great abuses of intelligence, which violate pure intellectuality as well as the sense of the sacred;[39] it is through this propensity that thinkers "are

---

[38] Within the framework of Christian art, the second image is nevertheless applicable to the flamboyant style of late Gothic art, in a relative manner and without abolishing the first. We take this opportunity to point out that the spiritual criterion beauty represents cannot apply to the neo-pagan art that poisoned Europe in the sixteenth century and that expresses the fatal marriage between religion and humanist civilizationism. No doubt, neither the cold and anthropolatrous gigantism of the Renaissance nor the morbid inflatedness of the Baroque prove anything against Catholicism in itself, but what they certainly prove is on the one hand that a religion which supports this language and expresses itself through it cannot have a monopoly of the absolute and exclusive Truth, and on the other hand that Catholicism, by this amalgam, exposed itself finally to being its victim; not in a total manner, which is excluded in advance, but nevertheless in an extremely serious manner. The humanization of the art—*a priori* divine—prefigured that of religion, at least of the official religion.

[39] By a curious and inevitable backlash, the abuse of intelligence is always accompanied by some logical inconsistency and some blindness: on the plane of art for example, it is illogical to copy nature when one is doomed in advance to stop halfway, since in painting, one can realize neither total perspective nor movement, any more than one can realize the latter in sculpture, not to mention the impossibility of imitating the living appearance of surfaces. Similarly in philosophy: by continuously forgetting that thought is there to furnish keys, and by continuously wanting to exhaust all the knowable by thought alone, one ends by no longer knowing how to think at all; and

wise in their own eyes" and end by "calling evil good, and good evil"
and by "putting darkness for light, and light for darkness" (Is. 5:20, 21);
they are also the ones who, on the plane of life or experience, "make
bitter what is sweet", namely the love of the eternal God, and "sweet
what is bitter", namely the illusion of the evanescent world.

One cannot understand the meaning of the divine Message without
knowing the nature of the human receptacle; he who understands
man, understands all the supernatural and cannot help but accept it.
Now man is made to contemplate the Absolute starting from contingency; the Absolute is conscious of itself in itself, but it also wishes
to be conscious of itself starting from an other than itself; this indirect
vision is a possibility necessarily included in the Infinitude belonging
to the Absolute. In consequence, it could not not be realized; it was
necessary that there be a world, beings, men. To contemplate the
Absolute starting from the contingent is correlatively to see things in
God and to see God in things, in such manner that they do not take us
away from God and that on the contrary they bring us closer to Him;
this is the *raison d'être* of man, and from it ensue existential rights as
well as spiritual duties. Man in principle has the right to the satisfac-
tion of his basic needs and to the enjoyment of a congenial ambience,
but he has this right only in view of his vocation of knowing God,
whence derives his duty to practice the disciplines that contribute
directly or indirectly to this knowledge.

The worth of man lies in his consciousness of the Absolute, and
consequently in the integrality and depth of this consciousness; having
lost sight of it by plunging himself into the world of phenomena
viewed as such—this is prefigured by the fall of the first couple—man
needs to be reminded of it by the celestial Message. This Message
comes finally from "himself", not of course from his empirical "I" but
from his immanent Selfhood, which is that of God and without which
there would be no "I", whether human, angelic, or other; the cred-

likewise for science, which out of principle bypasses everything essential, as is proved
moreover by its dismal results. Some will term our doctrine "dogmatic" and "naive",
which for us is a compliment.

ibility of the Message results from the fact that it is what we are, both within ourselves and beyond ourselves. In the depths of transcendence is immanence, and in the depths of immanence, transcendence.

It has been said that, if nothing can logically oblige a people to believe what a Prophet preaches to them, nothing can oblige the Prophet himself to believe what God reveals or seems to reveal to him; the lack of credibility would be the same in the one case as in the other. Now, apart from the fact that to be able to assess the matter it would be necessary either to be a Prophet or to hear a Prophet preach, the flaw of the opinion in question lies in its flagrant ignorance concerning the phenomenon of Revelation and that of faith, and then in begging the question by positing that there is no God; for if God is real, He necessarily finds a way to make Himself heard and make Himself accepted.

The fundamental solution to the problem of the credibility of religious axioms, and consequently the quintessence of the proofs of God, lies in the ontological correspondence between the macrocosm and the microcosm, that is, in the fact that the microcosm has to mirror the macrocosm; in other words, the subjective dimension, taken in its totality, coincides with the objective dimension, from which the religious and metaphysical truths derive in the first place. What matters is to actualize this coincidence, and this is what Revelation does, in principle or *de facto*, by awakening, if not always direct Intellection, at least the indirect Intellection which is Faith; *credo ut intelligam*.

All that we can know, we carry within ourselves, hence this is what we are; and that is why we can know it. This mystery could be symbolized by a circle comprising four poles: the lower pole would represent the human subject insofar as it is cut off from the object; the upper pole on the contrary would represent absolute Selfhood, which is neither subject nor object or which is both at once, or the one within the other. The right half of the circle would be the objective world, and the left half, subjective depth; in the center of each half, thus halfway towards Selfhood, would be situated respectively the absolute Object and the absolute Subject, or in other words, Selfhood indirectly perceived or experienced either as object or as subject. Now the circle is always the same Real; and that is why it is just as absurd to say that God does not exist since we have no objective perception of Him, as it is to say that He is absolutely unknowable because He is absolutely transcendent. For this transcendence, in the final analysis, is our own Essence and the foundation for our immortality.

The religious phenomenon comes down in the final analysis to a manifestation, both intellective and volitive, of the relationship between the Principle and its manifestation, or in other words, between the divine Substance and cosmic accidentality, or between *Ātmā* and *Samsāra*; and given that this relationship comprises diverse aspects, the religious phenomenon is diversified in accordance with these aspects or possibilities.

In the last analysis, every religion presents itself as a "myth" referring to a given "archetype", and thereby, but secondarily, to all archetypes; all these aspects are linked, but one alone determines the very form of the myth. If the Amidist perspective recalls the Christian perspective, that is because, within the framework of Buddhism, it refers more particularly to the archetype that determines Christianity; it is not because it was influenced by the latter, to say nothing of the historical impossibility of this hypothesis. Average man is incapable, not of conceiving the archetypes, no doubt, but of being interested in them; he has need of a myth that humanizes and dramatizes the archetype and that unleashes the corresponding reactions of the will and the sensibility; that is, average man, or collective man, has need of a god who resembles him.[40]

The Taoist *Yin-Yang* is an adequate image of the fundamental relationship between the Absolute and the contingent, God and the world, or God and man: the white part of the figure represents God, and the black part, man. The black dot in the white part is "man in God"—man principally prefigured in the divine order—or the relative in the Absolute, if this paradox is permissible, or the divine Word which in fact prefigures the human phenomenon; if cosmic

[40] Personal and dramatic in the case of Christianity; impersonal and serene in the case of Buddhism; the one being reflected sporadically in the other. We cite these two examples because of their disparity. Let us add that Arianism is a kind of interference, within Christianity, of the archetype-possibility of Islam, whereas inversely Shiism appears, within Islam, as an archetypal interference of Christian dramatism.

manifestation were not anticipated within the principial order, no world would be possible, nor any relationship between the world and God. Inversely and complementarily, the white dot in the black part of the *Yin-Yang* is the "human God", the "God-Man", which refers to the mystery of Immanence and to that of Theophany, hence also to that of Intercession and Redemption, or of the as it were "respiratory" reciprocity between earth and Heaven; if the latter were not present in the former, existence would vanish into nothingness, it would be impossible *a priori*. Herein lies the whole play of *Māyā* with its modes, degrees, cycles, diversity, and alternations.

On the one hand, the Principle alone is, manifestation—the world—is not; on the other hand, manifestation is real—or "not unreal"—by the fact, precisely, that it manifests, projects, or prolongs the Principle; the latter being absolute, hence for that very reason infinite, it requires by virtue of this very infinitude, the projection of itself in the "other than itself". On the one hand, the Principle has a tendency to "punish" or to "destroy" manifestation because the latter, as contingency, is not the Principle, or because it tends to be the Principle illusorily and with a luciferian intention; in short, because "God alone is"; on the other hand, the Principle "loves" manifestation and "remembers" that manifestation belongs to it, that manifestation is not "other than it", and it is within this ontological perspective that the mystery of Revelation, Intercession, Redemption is to be situated. In this manner the relationships between the Principle and manifestation give rise to diverse archetypes of which the religions are the mythical crystallizations that are predisposed so as to set into motion the will and the sensibility of given men and given human collectivities.

But the archetypes of the objective, macrocosmic, and transcendent order are also those of the subjective, microcosmic, and immanent order, the human Intellect coinciding—beyond individuality—with the universal Intellect; so much so that the revealed myth, even while coming in fact from the exterior and from the "Lord", comes in principle also from "ourselves", from the interior, and from the "Self". This is to say that the acceptance of the religious Message coincides, in principle and in depth, with the acceptance of what we are, in ourselves yet at the same time beyond ourselves; for there where immanence is, there is also the transcendence of the Immanent.

To believe in God is to become again what we are; to become it to the very extent that we believe, and that believing becomes being.

APPENDIX

Selections from Letters and
Other Previously Unpublished Writings

1

The institution of every tradition is operated through the Word by means of a principle, which, in Christianity, is represented by Saint Peter: we refer here to the principle of the formal realization of the tradition, a principle of which, within the framework of Christianity, Saint Peter was the human expression. To this principle is related another, namely, that of the expansion of the tradition, a principle represented by Saint Paul, whose investiture took place by means of the following words: "For this man is to me a vessel of election, to carry my name before the Gentiles and kings and the children of Israel" (Acts 9:15); and also: "Thou shalt be his witness to all men of those things which thou hast seen and heard" (Acts 22:15). As for the Johannine principle, this links the Christian tradition to the universal and primordial tradition; that is why there is a certain antinomy between it and the two preceding principles, which are subordinated to it, and this relative antinomy is none other than that of "form" and "spirit". This necessary, because inevitable, antinomy between John and Peter finds its expression in Christ's reproach to Peter on the subject of John (John 21:22), a reproach which indicates that these are things which do not enter the domain of Peter.

2

Another pitfall is the problem of conversions. First of all, it is not true that the one who changes religion for valid motives, "loses the benefit of what he has already obtained"; on the contrary, this something—the ineffaceable sacraments for example—will be turned to account within the framework of the new spiritual economy; and it is necessarily so because there is only one God, and because, precisely, the reasons for the change are valid; valid in the eyes of God before being valid in the eyes of men. I am thinking here of esoteric reasons, which exclude misinterpretation or contempt for the religion abandoned; the case is obviously different when there is "conversion" properly so called, for then the old religion is rejected and its ineffaceable traces, now incapable of being turned to account, are at least neutralized. All this has nothing to do with the question of knowing whether, yes or no, one has "transcended the limits of individuality"; there is no "quasi-mixture of forms", since the formal elements of the old religion, as I have said, are in part neutralized and in part revalued, or either one or the other. If it were not so, no religion could ask for conversion; no conversion could be preached; the Islamic preaching and the conversion of millions of Christians, Hindus, Africans, and Malays, would be illegitimate. And when Christian missionaries preach in all the countries that they can reach, they do not ask if the structure of a given religion—of Hinduism for example, with is various forms of initiation, its *samskāra*s and its *dīkshā*s—renders possible the conversion to Christianity, or if the candidates for baptism have reached the primordial state; from Antiquity onwards, Christians have baptized initiates of Eleusis, Samothrace, and elsewhere, without causing any difficulties. The Christian requirement is unconditional, and the same is true for every other "expansive" religion.

3

The question of Intercession derives from the eternal connections between the Principle and Manifestation; the "body transpierced" is an aspect of Manifestation in front of the Principle, but it is clearly not all of the aspects. The Taoist *Yin-Yang* is an adequate image of the relationship between the Absolute and the contingent, God and the world, or God and man: the white part is God, the black part is man; the black dot in the white part is "man in God"—principially prefigured in God—or the relative in the Absolute, or the Word, which in fact prefigures man; the white dot in the black part is the "human God", the "God-Man", which refers to the mystery of immanence. The four words of the *Shahādah*—and the two halves of this formula, *Nafy* and *Ithbāt*—lead to the same analysis.

On the one hand, the Principle alone is, Manifestation is not; on the other hand, Manifestation is real by the fact, precisely, that it manifests and thus prolongs the Principle. On the one hand, the Principle has the tendency to "punish" or to "destroy" Manifestation because it is not It, or because it seems to want to be It, or because It alone is; on the other hand, the Principle loves Manifestation and "remembers" that it is not "other than It", and it is in this perspective that the mystery of Intercession inserts itself, and also that of the mystery of Redemption. But it is false—while being exoterically admissible, the religions being *upāyas*—to maintain that between the Principle and Manifestation there is only one single relationship, or that man is reduced to a single possibility.

Meister Eckhart wrote some extremely bold formulations about all of this: for example, the distinction between "Godhead" (= Beyond-Being) and "God" (= Being) is like the distinction between Heaven and earth; Vedantists say analogous things about *Ātmā* and *Īshvara*, or *Para-Brahma* and *Brahma* or *Apara-Brahma* (= *nirguna* and *saguna*).

And these *haqā'iq* have to be emphasized when one writes as a metaphysician on the varied and complementary connections between God and the world; and on what other grounds could a metaphysician write about this if not by referring to the principial? For finally, if one is going to take the trouble to write, one must know why and for whom; one must kindle some light and seek to enlighten someone or other. And one must know on what grounds one stands.

4

Concentration in itself is not too difficult, but what is difficult is maintaining concentration in duration. I want to say that prayer has two extensions, one in space, and that is the easier one, and one in time, and that is the harder one; our existence is "world" and "life". And the first extension of prayer is that we free ourselves inwardly from the world, from multiplicity; the second is that this inward liberation become habitual; just as the world must become a point, the center where we stand or where our prayer or the Divine Name stands, so must our life become an instant, the now of God, through which duration flows simultaneously. God knows that we are weak, and does not expect any miracle from us; but the little that we can do for the next world can be infinitely meaningful.

5

All indirectly or directly necessary sensory experiences or activities, be they physical or psychic, have so to speak a sacramental value and a corresponding effectiveness, at least in principle; in the case of primordial man as well as the enlightened sage it is actual; indeed this results from the nature of things. Meister Eckhart said that he who has grasped this mystery—that is to say, he who has fully realized it— receives the Eucharist each time upon eating or drinking; this indicates the sacredness of food and of eating and drinking; that is why there are peoples or tribes who remain reverentially silent while eating, and therein also lies the deeper significance of grace pronounced at meal-time. The same applies to other sensory experiences that are noble in themselves, and it applies above all to love; and then, also to gazing and hearing, for both can be either worldly or holy, exteriorizing or interiorizing. Sacredness of what is natural; sanctification of what is natural; healing through the natural; therein lies the spiritual noble-ness of man. One can also say that this nobleness is reverential devo-tion; hence, the direct or indirect remembrance of God, *dhikru 'Llāh*. Gratitude is connected to that because the noble man does not allow habituation to jade him, he always experiences the symbol and beauty anew, as upon the first day of the encounter; hence his soul does not age, it remains in timeless childhood and becomes ever truer to itself.

6

Given that God is omnipresent and therefore manifests Himself also in particular ways, man must always be aware of this divine proximity; this is the sense of the sacred. Most men lack this sense, or they rel-egate the sacred to a quite limited domain, remote from their lives, and live altogether outside its perfume. The sense of the sacred is con-nected with the sense of dignity; one must be mindful of both in the spiritual life; dignity is the manifestation of the motionless Center in the sphere of motion, and thus is a manner of remembrance of God. I emphasize this point because we live in a world of profanity and lack of dignity and because there is a risk that many pious men do not suffi-ciently heed what seem like insignificant manifestations of these vices.

7

Here we are still in winter, or almost; we had a heavy snowfall several days ago. Our street is like a construction site, and since it is raining all the time, if it is not snowing, one sinks into mud. Nowadays, one does not make a road because one needs a road, but one convinces oneself that one needs one because, for political (electoral), economic (the industrial juggernaut), and for philosophical reasons (evolutionist dynamism), one thinks that one has to build something.

8

Concupiscence is neither the desire for enjoyment in itself, nor enjoyment as such, but both inasmuch as they are situated outside of God and therefore are no longer supports for spiritual contemplation, nor concrete contemplative participations in divine Beatitude; on the contrary, enjoyment when separated from God—because of the Fall—takes one away from God owing to the fact that it appears as an end in itself; it is practically speaking an idol, on the one hand, since it replaces God and, on the other hand, it puffs up gross individuality; there is therefore something luciferian about it. Before the Fall, the desire for carnal union coincided with a spiritual desire, that is to say with the desire for a particular perception of the Infinite or, formulated differently, with a desire for extinction in the consciousness of the Divine; this primordial point of view, if one may say, is always accessible in principle on the basis of a certain esoteric sanctity, as is proven above all by examples such as Krishna, David, Solomon, Muhammad.

Regarding marriage in Christianity, there can be no reference here to an ideal couple; the Christ and the Virgin do not constitute a couple. There remains Joseph and the Virgin, then the Holy Spirit and the Virgin; now Joseph cannot be the model, precisely, of a husband, and as for the Holy Spirit, which husband would dare put himself in its place? And which husband would dare touch—in imagination— the Holy Virgin? The model of the Christian marriage is either the relationship between Christ and his Church, or the love of the soul for its Creator, or for the divine Infinitude; in this case, the partner— male or female—takes on a mystical symbolism, an example of which is given to us by the troubadours; the case of the *Fedeli d'Amore* is no doubt analogous.

9

Can one speak of the "Poverty" of God, or—which amounts to the same—of the "Poverty" of a Hypostasis? I say no, because poverty is something privative, and no privation can be attributed to God; it is true that one can speak of the "Divine Void" and of "Non-Being", but these are notions which, while being negative, are neutral, and in any case have nothing human about them; the void in itself, especially that of space, is in its manner a good and does not suggest any prejudicial privation; the non-existence of an evil is not itself an evil merely for the fact of being a negation.

Instead of "Poverty", one should have said "Simplicity"; for simplicity is a quality and not a privation. And I must say right away that I am against all sentimental, imaginative, humanizing, and psychologizing drama when speaking of realities in the divine order; even while admitting that in this matter there are a few honorable precedents, these do not constitute norms, and one should not imitate them. I repeat that to be void is simply not to be full, whatever the value or non-value of any imaginable content may be, whereas to be poor is to lack something; God lacks nothing.[1]

Alongside the Simplicity of God, which is inexhaustible richness, there is divine Charity, which is inexhaustible Life; one could call it the divine Generosity, namely (according to Saint Augustine) the innate tendency of the Good to impart itself, and thus to radiate *in divinis*, and even into the darkness of our fallen world.

---

[1] Olier says in his *Introduction to Christian Life and Virtues*: "The most worship-worthy Persons of the Holy Trinity are infinitely rich and blessed in their possession of the Divine Essence. . . . God is so perfect, and encompasses in Himself all the advantages of His creature with such an eminence and plenitude, that His very least possession and joy lets us taste every possible kind of good, so that those who possess it, be it on earth or in Heaven, find in it all their joy, all their contentment, all their repose, and all their beatitude."

10

It is known that theology distinguishes in the Trinity the "Essence" and the "relations"; the Essence is that which concerns God as such, and which consequently is capable of no internal differentiation whatsoever, while the relations are that which, without having any effect on the immutable Essence, differentiates the three Divine Persons; these relations consist in what theology calls the "relations of origin"; that is to say, the Father, who is "unbegotten", is Principle in relation to the Son, whom He "begets"; the Father and Son are in turn Principle in relation to the Holy Spirit, who proceeds from them like a "gift", or who, according to the Greeks, proceeds from the Father and is "delegated" by—rather than proceeding from—the Son.[2]

Metaphysically, these "relations of origin" refer to the fundamental degrees of divine Reality, or, inversely, that is to say, starting from the Father, they refer to the fundamental degrees of divine Determination by which God, in His desire to know Himself or to realize Himself

---

[2] As regards the divergences between Latins and Greeks, we would maintain that the two opposing conceptions are equally true, as always happens in the case of what one might call "extrinsic heresies", that is to say, of doctrines which are themselves orthodox, but which appear "heretical" in relation to another equally orthodox doctrine; thus, the *filioque* of the Latins is justified since the Father has nothing that He does not share with the Son, and on the other hand, the rejection of the *filioque* by the Greeks is justified because the Son, as such, is not the Father. Their distinction is affirmed precisely by the different modes of "procession" of the Holy Spirit: the Holy Spirit "proceeds" from the Son in so far as the Son is God, but he is only "delegated" by the Son in so far as the latter is an "internal mode" of the Divinity, so that the "delegation" of the Holy Spirit is nothing other than a mode of his "procession" from God. Saint John of Damascus expressly affirms: "We say that the Holy Spirit proceeds from the Father, and we call him Spirit of the Father; we in no wise say that the Spirit proceeds from the Son, but only that he is the Spirit of the Son." To say that the Holy Spirit also proceeds from the Son amounts in a certain sense to saying that the Son is the Father; if the Latins have not hesitated to attribute the procession of the Spirit to the Son also, it is because, inasmuch as Essence, the Son is indeed identical with the Father. We say "inasmuch as Essence", and not "inasmuch as God", because, as we shall see presently, God is not only Essence, but comprises "modes" or "degrees", or in theological language, "Persons"; the term "Essence" consequently does not designate the whole divine Reality, otherwise the Trinity would not be God.

Let us note here that religious schisms—which must not be confused with heresies in an absolute sense—always arise from the inability of the religious point of view to synthesize two divergent but complementary perspectives within the framework of one and the same integral truth.

in distinctive mode, determines Himself, or rather "His Self".[3] This manner of regarding the Persons of the Trinity as degrees of Reality, or as divine Determinations, causes a certain pre-eminence of the Father in relation to the Son, and of the Father and Son taken together in relation to the Holy Spirit, a pre-eminence which, although occurring only in connection with the degrees of Reality or Determination and in no wise with the one and indivisible Essence, does not enter into the perspective of theology, for the simple reason that the specifically religious point of view does not conceive the degrees of the Essence, since these degrees seem to threaten—at least from an anthropomorphist point of view—the unity and indivisibility of the latter. It is here that, in order to introduce the Trinity into exoterism, one encounters the paradoxical character, not of the Trinity itself, of course, but of its translation into dogma. One is obliged, on pain of saying nothing at all, to make explicit its modes of differentiation; but on the other hand, in order not to slip into esoterism—a domain to which the Trinitarian conception essentially belongs and towards which it logically, or rather ontologically, tends—one is obliged to interrupt at the decisive moment the chain of ideas which leads directly to esoterism and to return without transition to the initial affirmation that the Essence is one, an affirmation which in no way answers the question regarding the meaning of the differences of the Persons. Thus it is said that the Father possesses Divinity as Principle, while the Son possesses it by birth; or that the Father is Light, Life, and Wisdom as Source, while the Son is such as river or outflow; or that the Father is generator of Greatness, while the Son is himself Greatness; one concludes that the Father and the Son differ, but one hastens to add, in order to annul *a priori* the consequences implied by this conclusion and in order to exclude everything that might transcend the exoteric dimension required by dogmatization, that they do not differ by Essence, but only by origin; one then seems not to know that "origin", short of being purely and simply a nothingness, must in the nature of things represent an aspect of Essence, that is to say, something which is *ad*

---

[3] According to a *hadīth*, David asked God: "Where wast Thou, O Lord, before creation?" God replied: "I was a hidden treasure; I wanted to be known, and I created the world in order to be known." This may also be applied to the internal differentiations of the divine Principle, which are so many determinations of the divine Essence: this Essence is Non-Being (or Beyond-Being), but its determinations engender Being and Existence.

se and not *ad alterum*; to say that each Divine Person possesses an Essence of His own, which represents His origin, is not to deny the Essence which "subsists" in what can be called "the Essence of the Person", for this latter is a mode of the One Essence.

11

The (authentic) metaphysician, or the (integral, not partial) esoterist, considers everything under the aspect of: 1. the metaphysical distinction between the Absolute and the relative; 2. the sincere, profound, and quasi-permanent concentration on the Absolute.

Therefore he will ask, when faced with a particular religious element, or a particular religious fact, or this or that historical, mythological, symbolic, ritual phenomenon or other: what does this mean with respect to the distinction between the relative and the Absolute; with respect to spiritual concentration? Or again: with respect to transcendence, or with respect to immanence? And finally: with respect to the conformity of the soul, or with our participation in divine Beauty ("Be ye therefore perfect, even as your Father which is in heaven is perfect"); hence with respect to intrinsic virtue, to the fundamental virtues?

Hence the true esoterist will not enclose himself in the phenomenal order of religion; things have no interest in themselves, that is to say outside of the connections that we have just pointed out; the vertical takes precedence over the horizontal. For example, there is no need to explore historically and psychologically, and forever starting anew, different incidents in the life of Christ or of the Virgin; it is enough to grasp what their metaphysical and mystical meanings are, assuming that one really feels the need to deepen them; in most cases such incidents relate aspects or states—of proximity or of distance— of the soul before God, unless they have another meaning that is literal and made explicit by the words themselves. At all events, one may have the vocation to want to understand a particular religious phenomenon, but one is not obliged to understand everything; we must grasp what is essential and accept that there are things that we do not understand in depth; it is not that these things are out of reach by their nature, but it is neither possible nor therefore indispensable that man know everything, or reflect on everything; let him therefore keep *a priori* to what is essential and he shall see what happens afterwards. If a man is quasi-perfect in his understanding and practice of the essential, he will know what "God asks of him", in other words, what he must take into consideration additionally; but if he does not concern himself sufficiently with what is essential, all the rest will become for him a temptation for dispersion, and also for contraction and for getting bogged-down, all the more as a person risks lacking competence, precisely, in the measure he neglects intellectually or spiritually what is essential about the doctrine and the method; that is to say, in the measure that he underestimates theoretically or practically what gives meaning to all the rest.

To repeat, or to specify: there are three elements to consider: 1. divine Absoluteness; 2. human Concentration; 3. Perfection, or Beauty, at once divine and human. That is everything. The essence of Perfection, or of Virtue, is the sense of the Sacred, or Adoration, Devotion; and therefore everything that is both their condition and their result, namely: detachment (with regard to the world and to oneself), vigilance, gratitude, generosity; or patience, fervor, contentment, trust. Resignation and faith; and with faith, joy.

12

The sentences in *From the Divine to the Human* mean: Christianity does not possess an official metaphysical doctrine which every Christian metaphysician would be obliged to accept and which at the same time would be contrary to all the non-Christian metaphysical doctrines.

The question is not whether a metaphysical doctrine—such as the Five Divine Presences—"should be" imposed on all Christians; who would impose it? The question is only that Christianity does not possess a metaphysical system which the Church imposes *ex cathedra*.

The theory of the Five Presences cannot be designated as "the transcendent unity of religions". But since this theory is intrinsically true and metaphysically necessary, it is evidently known to all Christian metaphysicians, under a certain terminology. Every Christian knows that there is matter and psychism, then that there is the heavenly world which transcends both; and Meister Eckhart distinguishes sharply between the personal God (*Gott*) and the impersonal Godhead or Divinity (*Gottheit*).

The Five Presences are not a manner of "reducing the Absolute to a given relative aspect of the Real"; they are a description of the onto-cosmological structure of the Universe; they do not mean that other aspects of the universal Reality do not exist, and their particularity has nothing to do with a conceptual relativity.

It is evident that the transcendent unity of religions includes more than just the hierarchy of universal Reality.

The Christian metaphysician does not necessarily "reduce" the *Vedānta* to the Holy Trinity; but he may perceive the *Vedānta* in the framework of this dogma, or he may express his Vedantic intuitions in Christian terms.

13

If one really knew that God is God, and that only God is God, then one would know everything else. Therefore, whenever the juggling tricks of the world cause doubts about this or that to arise in us, we must take refuge in the all-truth that God is Reality. It would indeed be strange if we knew and understood all possibilities from the outset. On the plane of phenomena—which is also the plane of darkness and therefore of contradiction—to see through all the artifices of *Māyā* on this plane from the outset would simply not be human.

Firstly, we must find our joy in God, not in the world; it follows from this that we must not be disappointed if we do not find our joy in the world.

Secondly, we must surrender ourselves to God, and judge the world from the standpoint of this surrender. We must not let the absurdity of the world sap our blood so that we are turned away from our surrender to God.

Thirdly, we must not forget that the evil enemy provokes absurdity in order to bewilder us and turn us away from God. Our surrender must not, cannot, depend on our understanding all riddles; it is unconditional, depending only on the Truth of truths. Surrender to God was there before the existence of the world, and before we ourselves existed. We do not create it, we enter into it; it is our deep, eternal Being.

Our trust in God must protect us from doubts about the world; it must be stronger than all absurdity. Otherwise it would be as if we had doubts about the Truth of truths, whereas in fact this Truth is our real Being.

Pure Truth, pure Being, pure Inwardness.

The Mystery of Numbers

Metaphysical realities are expressed *a priori* by concepts and words; they can also be expressed by symbolisms such as forms and numbers and then, less fundamentally, by the indefinitely varied and particular symbolisms of virgin Nature and human art.

If the "metaphysical writing" of Pythagoras is expressed by numbers and not by geometric forms, this is because the forms are "concrete", and the numbers "abstract": when we say "triangle", an image is evoked, whereas when we say "three", nothing overly imaginable is indicated; it will be said without hesitation that God is "one"—this does not harm His transcendence—but one would not dream of qualifying Him as "circular" or "spherical".

The Pythagorean numbers prove that number in itself is not synonymous with quantity pure and simple, for they are essentially qualitative; they are so to the degree that they are close to Unity, their point of departure. The principle of quantity, inasmuch as it is opposed to that of quality, intervenes only to the extent that a number becomes distant from its roots and is lost in undifferentiation and the insignificant; let us not forget, however, that ordered quantity also possesses a qualitative aspect: the numbers one hundred and one thousand, for example, have a consonance of majesty; and age, the number of years, is venerable. Unity and Totality meet.

Each number has its cosmic image: after the images of duality—such as man and woman—there are the three dimensions of space; the four cardinal points, then the four phases of the temporal cycle, namely morning, day, evening, night, or spring, summer, autumn, winter, or again childhood, youth, maturity, old age; for the number five, there are the elements, the senses, the fingers; all told, five signifies one "substance" with four "functions".[1] All these images have their prototypes in the universal Order.

One might wonder if Unity is really a number; strictly speaking, number begins only with Duality, which opens the door to that projection of the Infinite which is the indefinite. Nonetheless, to speak of

---

[1] According to Islamic angelology, the "Spirit", *Rūh*, is more or less an emanation of God; it is assisted by four Archangels, who are so to speak the pillars of the world.

Unity is to speak of Totality; in other words, Unity signifies the absolute Real, and likewise with Totality, which represents the Real in all its ontological "extent"; Reality and All-Possibility meet.

That which is not inexistent is real according to the degree and the mode that God has assigned to it; God being the Real in itself, He who is "That I am". Now the Real, not being nothing, is everything: which is to say that radiation is in the nature of Being, whence All-Possibility and the inexhaustible diversity it implies. It is in the nature of the Good to impart itself, according to Plato; and the Real is the Sovereign Good, *to Agathon*, from which derive all Heavenly and earthly goods.

Clearly, Unity is the first principle that penetrates and regulates universal Manifestation, in the sense that on the one hand it projects its reflections everywhere, and on the other hand brings phenomena back to Unity, symbolically at least. In this regard, Unity tends everywhere to overcome Duality, of which it is nevertheless the ontological origin: thus, masculinity and femininity seem to form an irreducible bipolarity; but Unity reminds us that this duality has its reason for being *a priori* in Love, which wishes to manifest itself and hence is obliged by its very nature to do so, and *a posteriori* in the child, who is the fruit of the bipolarization. Unity also indicates to us this truth: it is only in a certain respect that the terms of a duality, such as the masculine and the feminine, are complementary; in another respect—that of essential Reality—each of the terms is unique, which is to say that the supreme Principle can be envisaged under a feminine aspect as well as under a masculine aspect. Another example is that of the bipolarity of subject and object: under the influence of the principle of Unity, the subject isolates itself and becomes a manifestation of the unique Self, thus of the divine Subject, which obviously has no partner; and similarly, *mutatis mutandis*, for the pole object, which isolates itself and becomes a participative reflection of divine Being, thus of the objective aseity of the Real. Yet the bipolarity, whatever its kind, is not abolished, it is simply "interiorized", in the sense that—in conformity with the principle of *Yin-Yang*—each of the two poles in its way contains the other; moreover, if this were not so, there would be no possibility of contact between them, for two absolutely different things could never understand one another and collaborate. If there were not in woman an element of masculinity, nor in man an element of femininity, there could never be unity between them.

It must be emphasized: the subject may be without relation to outward objects, but by compensation it bears the element object within itself, in the sense that pure subjectivity potentially contains the metaphysical essence of the knowable; this isolation and this compensation are realized on the one hand in deep sleep and on the other hand in concentration on the Void, *vacare Deo*; now the Void is unique, it is in a certain sense the essence of all possible objects, inasmuch as it coincides mystically with the Presence of the absolute "Other", at once transcendent and immanent. Correlatively, we will say that the object in itself realizes subjectivity by the forms or other characteristics it assumes; without this immanence of the subjective or of the "individual", the object would be an undifferentiated substance. It is the element "subjectivity"—we do not say "consciousness"—that coagulates and differentiates the "objective" and *a priori* "formless" substance; if fire, water, gold, lead are what they are, it is in virtue of a material "individuality" or "originality", and this is independent of the subsequent heavenly projection that introduces into the earthly substance subjectivity properly so called, namely life and consciousness.[2]

It follows from all we have just said that the "object" does not always coincide with the "known", any more than the "subject" necessarily coincides with the "knower"; this is so only in respect to cognition, but not when one envisages an object in itself, or the subject in itself, hence in their aseity. Outside the cognitive act, the subject is that which is capable of knowing, and the object, that which is knowable; hence the "conscious" on the one hand and the "real" on the other—the real being what it is, whether we perceive it or not. In the act of knowing, the subject and the object are, by definition as it were, inseparable; but the fact that in this case the one requires the other does not signify that the two poles always meet *de facto*, otherwise there would not be planets that no living being has ever seen, nor consciousnesses capable of emptying themselves of all infiltration

---

[2] Which is to say that the celestial prototypes—the Platonic "ideas"—descend, through several cosmic planes, towards the material plane, in which they become "incarnated" successively according to a logical order; life and consciousness could not arise from matter by "horizontal" evolution.

from without; what this inseparability means fundamentally is that the subject by definition is capable of knowing, and that the object is susceptible of being known. In God, the Subject and the Object, the Masculine and the Feminine, Transcendence and Immanence, coincide; likewise for the pure Intellect, which being *aliquid increatum et increabile*, belongs to the divine Order.

It is curious to note—be it said in passing—that the word "objectivity" signifies a moral quality, with good reason moreover, whereas the word "subjectivity" wrongly signifies a defect; the defect clearly exists, and more so than ever, but it ought to be designated by the term "subjectivism". As for the term "objectivism", which is not in use, it could designate the tendency—likewise all too widespread—of living only towards the outward and through the outward; which in our day is the norm, whence the absence of an appropriate term. The word "objectivity" signifies, all told, "conformity to the nature of things", independently of all interference of individual tendencies or tastes; the word "subjectivity", for its part, ought to designate the contemplative withdrawal into the "heart", given that "the kingdom of God is within you". For man, the reason for the existence of outward values is spiritual interiorization: in the direction of the Real which we can encounter and attain to only within ourselves, in our transpersonal center. But this is possible solely in virtue of our consciousness of the Transcendent, which is the ultimate Essence of all "objective" values, while at the same time having its seat in the depths of the Heart-Intellect. *Tat tvam asi*: "That art thou".

— ·⁝· —

One and the same number may represent either a diversity of functions or a hierarchy of values, depending on whether the symbolism is "horizontal" or "vertical": the relationship between the Principle and manifestation is not the same as that between the subject and the object; the Ternary *Sat-Chit-Ānanda*—Being-Consciousness-Bliss—which pertains to the divine Order, represents a different structure than the Ternary *sattva-rajas-tamas*—ascending, expansive, and descending tendencies—which applies to the realm of *Māyā*.

The perspectives are diverse, for one cannot reduce universal Possibility to one or two formulas. After Unity must come Duality, and after Duality, Trinity, and so on; one numerical mystery leads to another. Thus, it is in the nature of Unity to tend towards an extrinsic overflowing: there where God is, there also will be the world. And it is in the nature of Duality to wish to be delivered from its aspect of division, and this transcending—or this solution—occurs either *a priori* or *a posteriori*: the division masculinity-femininity has its so to speak causal reason for being in the mystery of love, but from another point of view, the opposition of the sexes finds its solution in that third element which is the child. Duality is as if suspended between two Unities, one initial and principial and the other terminal and manifested. And likewise, *mutatis mutandis*, with the opposition subject-object: the two terms find their solution, on the one hand in Knowledge as such, which is union and not division, and on the other hand in given instances of knowledge, which are satisfied in themselves and are not concerned with their instrumental or operative cause. Every even number tends toward manifestation; every odd number denotes a return to the Principle, and this, in both cases, according to a perspective that is more and more complex and tending in the direction of diversity and specificity.

In regard to duality or bipolarity on the simply logical or dialectical plane, a clarification is called for here: it is important to distinguish between dualities that bring two complementary poles face to face and those that simply juxtapose a thing and its absence. The masculine and the feminine, activity and passivity, subject and object are complementary; but evil is not a complement of the good, any more than nothingness is a complement of Being. Altogether different, for example, is the opposition between activity and passivity, for the latter is not just a lack of the former; on the contrary it possesses its own qualities, its receptivity and gratitude.

If we have elaborated at such length on the problem of Duality and related questions, it is because in the realm of number, Duality is crucial in the sense that it is like a "creative explosion": at once a revelation, a point of departure, a fall. The great mystery is not in *Ātmā*, it is in *Māyā*; in Relativity, not in the Absolute.

The number Three, for its part, has about it something messianic; with Three, everything so to speak returns to order; it is the great Consolation, the new Golden Age. But "the die is cast", Duality must reappear; no longer as a sort of ontological cataclysm—our expressions are perhaps too imaginative—but as a new order, either "spatial" or "temporal", for there are the cardinal points just as there are the cycles of duration, symbolically speaking. Which is to say that the number four takes up again the function of the number two, but on a new basis, more stable in a certain sense but no less dramatic, if one may thus express it; and so on *ad infinitum*. This is the meaning of the alternation of the odd and even numbers—the point of departure being Duality—which progress towards a transnumerical Totality, within us and around us; towards the Apocatastasis as well as towards the extinction that is our profound meeting with God, beyond the servitudes of Contingency or Relativity. Number is the perspective of *Māyā*, within us as within the divine Order; "I am black, but beautiful".

Islam expresses the same mystery of innumerable—hence transnumerical—number by teaching that on the one hand God is One, but that on the other hand He has ninety-nine Names; now it is significant that here multitude is not expressed by the number one hundred: instead the symbolism stops at ninety-nine, an indecisive number; which expresses an ineffable transcendence. We find the same mystery in that altogether fundamental Text, the *Sūrah* of "Purification", *Ikhlās*, where the word "impenetrable", *samad*, is the complement of the word "one", *ahad*, with precisely the intention of expressing the limitless, at once transcendent and absolute: "Say: God is One; God is impenetrable; He begetteth not nor is He begotten; and there is none like unto Him."

EDITOR'S NOTES

Numbers in bold indicate pages in the text for which the following citations and explanations are provided.

Foreword

xi: The author's *Logique et Transcendance* (Paris: Éditions Traditionnelles, 1970) first appeared in English as *Logic and Transcendence*, translated by Peter N. Townsend (London: Perennial Books, 1975; New York: Harper & Row, 1975), and subsequently in a new translation by Mark Perry, Jean-Pierre Lafouge, and James S. Cutsinger as *Logic and Transcendence: A New Translation with Selected Letters*, edited by James S. Cutsinger (Bloomington, IN: World Wisdom, 2009); *Forme et Substance dans les Religions* (Paris: Dervy Livres, 1975) appeared in English as *Form and Substance in the Religions*, translated by Mark Perry and Jean-Pierre Lafouge (Bloomington, IN: World Wisdom, 2002); while *L'Esotérisme comme Principe et comme Voie* (Paris: Dervy Livres, 1978) appeared in English as *Esoterism as Principle and as Way* (London: Perennial Books, 1981).

Consequences Resulting from the Mystery of Subjectivity

3: The Latin *cogito ergo sum*, "I think; therefore I am", is found in the French philosopher René Descartes' (1596-1650) *Principles of Philosophy* (1644). In *Cartesian* philosophy the very act of thinking is the proof of the certainty of consciousness; it is therefore the sole initial truth immune from any doubt and danger of deception, capable of being the foundation for all other knowledge. In response to Descartes, the author has asserted that the German philosopher Franz von Baader's (1765-1841) "formula, *cogitor, ergo cogito et sum*, 'I am thought (by God); therefore I think, and I am' . . . is a pertinent expression of the causal or ontological relationship" between God and man because it highlights the status of human consciousness as both product and reflection of Divine consciousness (*Logic and Transcendence: A New Translation with Selected Letters*, ed. James S. Cutsinger [Bloomington, IN: World Wisdom, 2009], p. 38).

"*In the beginning* God created the heaven and the earth. And the earth was without form, and void; and darkness was upon the face of the deep. And *the Spirit* of God moved upon the face of the waters" (Gen. 1:1-2).

Transformist evolution, postulated by naturalist Charles Darwin (1809-1882) in his *Origin of Species* (1859), claims a transformation of one species into another through random evolutionary mutations and adaptations.

4: By *Intellection*, or intellectual intuition, the author refers to the direct and supra-rational recognition of a given truth. Elsewhere he clarifies that "Reflection, like intellection, is an activity of the intelligence, with the difference that in the second case this activity springs from that immanent divine spark that is the Intellect, whereas in the first case the activity starts from the reason, which is capable only of logic and not of intellective intuition" (*Sufism: Veil and Quintessence: A New Translation with Selected Letters*, ed. James S. Cutsinger [Bloomington, IN: World Wisdom, 2006], p. 17).

Intellection and Revelation are "supernaturally natural" to man in that they are constitutive of his human nature while having their roots in his divine supra-nature. The author remarks elsewhere that "Pure Intellection is a subjective and immanent Revelation just as Revelation properly so called is an objective and transcendent Intellection" (*Logic and Transcendence: A New Translation with Selected Letters*, ed. James S. Cutsinger [Bloomington, IN: World Wisdom, 2009], p. 26).

5: According to the ancient Greek philosopher *Plato* (427-347 B.C.), "seeking and learning are in fact nothing but recollection" (*Meno*, 81d), all knowledge being the result of an *archetypal remembrance*.

"It *must needs* be that *offenses come;* but woe to that man by whom the offence cometh" (Matt. 18:7).

By *rationalist luciferianism* the author refers to the reductionism of rationalist philosophers such as René Descartes and Immanuel Kant (1724-1804), who give reason pre-eminence over the Intellect. This *fall* of the intelligence is likened to the angel Lucifer, who turned *against God* and fell from heaven (cf. Is. 14:12-15).

Note 2: By *existentialist luciferianism* the author refers to the reductionism of existentialist philosophers such as Søren Kierkegaard (1813-1855) and Jean-Paul Sartre (1905-1980), who give human experience pre-eminence over the Intellect.

7: Note 5: The pronouncement "*Know thyself*" (*Gnothi seauton*), carved into the lintel of Apollo's Temple at Delphi, is the most famous of the *Delphic* oracles or *mysteries*.

8: "*I am black, but beautiful,* O ye daughters of Jerusalem, as the tents of

Kedar, as the curtains of Solomon" (Song of Sol. 1:5).

9: "I am *Alpha* and *Omega*, the *beginning* and the end, the first and the last" (Rev. 22:13).

Aspects of the Theophanic Phenomenon of Consciousness

12: Note 3: The Latin adage, *In vino veritas*, "In wine the truth", is attributed to the Roman historian Pliny the Elder (first century A.D.) and, in its earlier Greek version, to the Greek poet *Alcaeus* of Mytilene (sixth century B.C.).

The poet *Theocritus* (third century B.C.) was the father of Greek bucolic poetry. In his works the relationship between *intoxication* and divine *truth* is evoked through the influence of Dionysus, the Greek god of wine and ecstasy.

Note 4: Muhyi ad-Din *Ibn Arabi* (1165-1240), author of numerous works including *Meccan Revelations* and *Bezels of Wisdom*, was a prolific and profoundly influential Sufi mystic, known in tradition as the *Shaykh al-Akbar*, that is, the "great master".

The *troubadours* were medieval minstrels and lyric poets whose verse, composed in the old Occitan language, was dedicated to the *cult of the Lady*.

The *Fedeli d'Amore*, or "liegemen of love", were a group of medieval poets, including Dante, who transposed the courtly ideal of love for the earthly beloved—in Dante's case, Beatrice—into a means of deepening their love for God.

13: Meister *Eckhart* (c. 1260-1327), a German Dominican writer, was regarded by the author as the greatest of Christian metaphysicians and esoterists. His saying, *"The more he blasphemes the more he praises God"* is one of the twenty-eight articles condemned by the papal bull *In agro dominico* in 1329.

15: *Credo ut intelligam*, a Latin phrase meaning "I believe so that I may understand", is a maxim of Anselm of Canterbury (c. 1033-1109) who prefaced his ontological argument for the existence of God with the sentence: "I do not seek to understand so that I may believe; but I believe so that I may understand" (*Proslogion*, 1).

Transcendence Is Not Contrary to Sense

18: *Without this complexity there would be no world; to deny it would amount to maintaining that the Absolute is deprived of the dimension of Infinitude*: The author's most common exposition of universal metaphysics begins with a characterization of the supreme Reality as Absolute, Infinite, and Perfect: "On the hand, the Absolute is 'necessary' Being, that which must be, which cannot not be, and which for that very reason is unique; on the other hand, the Infinite is 'free' Being, which is limitless and which contains all that can be, and which for that very reason is total. This reality, absolute and infinite, necessary and free, unique and total, is *ipso facto* perfect: for it lacks nothing, and it possesses in consequence all that is positive; it suffices unto itself. This means that the Absolute, as well as the Infinite which is as it were its intrinsic complement or its *shakti*, coincides with Perfection; the Sovereign Good is the very substance of the Absolute" (*Survey of Metaphysics and Esoterism* [Bloomington, IN: World Wisdom, 2000], p. 26).

Note 3: For *Meister Eckhart* see editor's note for Ch. "Aspects of the Theophanic Phenomenon of Consciousness", p. 13.

19: Note 4: Abu al-Hasan al-*Ashari* (873-935), an important early Muslim theologian, insisted that God may appear *unjust* to our limited understanding because His All-Powerfulness defies human intelligence.

20: *Made in the image of God*: "And God said, Let us make man in our image, after our likeness" (Gen. 1:26).

For *Plato* see editor's note to Ch. "Consequences Resulting from the Mystery of Subjectivity", p. 5.

Aristotle (384-322 B.C.) was an ancient Greek philosopher whose works had a profound influence on the western intellectual tradition, including Christian *Scholastics* such as Thomas Aquinas.

The French mathematician, physicist, and Christian philosopher, Blaise *Pascal* (1623-1662), argued in his *Pensées* (1669) that when presented with an alternative between a finite and an infinite reality, reason commands that we *wager* in favor of the infinite. Therefore, to the question of whether or not God exists, one should always *wager* that He exists.

22: By *the logic of the pure metaphysician—of the Platonic or Vedantic type*, the author refers to perspectives such as Platonism or *Advaita Vedānta*, which view logic and rationality as instrumental to knowledge and its expression, but not as identifiable with supreme knowledge itself.

Gregory Palamas (c. 1296-1359), a monk of Mount Athos, is best known for his defense of the contemplative practices employed by the Hesychast Fathers, and for his distinction *in divinis* between the *Essence* and the *"Energies"*.

Note 8: *The "Byzantine" controversy on the unknowablity of God* was a fifth-sixth century theological debate over the divine Essence's unknowability, a central principle of Eastern Christian theology (see p. 44, Note 7 for additional remarks by the author on God's "unknowability").

Note 9: *Beyond-Being and Being:* Elsewhere the author remarks that "Beyond-Being—or Non-Being—is Reality absolutely unconditioned, while Being is Reality insofar as It determines Itself in the direction of its manifestation and in so doing becomes personal God" (*Stations of Wisdom* [Bloomington, IN: World Wisdom, 1995], p. 13n). Gregory Palamas' uncreated *Energies* refer to the determinative, creative, and deifying powers of the Divine, hence to *Being*.

23: *"God became man, in order that man might become God"*: The essential teaching expressed by this patristic formula is common to many *Fathers of the Church*, including Irenaeus (c. 130-c. 200), according to whom "the Son of God became the Son of man so that man, by entering into communion with the Word and thus receiving divine sonship, might become a son of God" (*Against Heresies*, 3:19); and Athanasius (c. 296-373), who wrote, "The Son of God became man in order that we might become God" (*On the Incarnation*, 54:3).

24: "Then David said to the Philistine, You come to me with a sword and with a spear and with a javelin; but I come to you in the name of the *Lord of hosts*, the God of the armies of Israel, whom you have defied" (1 Sam 17:45).

The *Christian* Apostles' *creed* begins, "I believe *in God, the all-powerful Father, creator of heaven and earth*" (Art. 1).

25: *Shankara* (788-820), the pre-eminent exponent of the classical Hindu school of metaphysical non-dualism or *Advaita Vedānta*, was regarded by the author as the greatest of all Hindu metaphysicians.

Ramanuja (1017-c. 1137) is widely regarded as the classic representative of *Vishishta Advaita*, that is, the Hindu *darshana* or perspective of "qualified non-dualism", in which emphasis is placed on the personal nature of God.

Platonic idealism teaches that the visible things of this world are but shadows or copies of invisible and eternal "Forms" or "Ideas", which themselves reflect the supreme reality of the Good.

Aristotelian hylomorphism teaches that individual substances are comprised of "matter" (*hyle*) and intelligible "form" (*morphe*).

"Though I speak with the tongues of men and of angels, and have not charity, I am become *as sounding brass, or a tinkling cymbal*" (1 Cor. 13:1).

26: *God created him "in His image"*: "And God said, Let us make man in our image, after our likeness" (Gen. 1:26).

Note 12: "*Folly in the eyes of the world*": "If any man among you seemeth to be wise in this world, let him become a fool, that he may be wise. For the wisdom of this world is foolishness with God" (1 Cor. 3:18-19).

The Interplay of the Hypostases

31: For *Plato* see editor's note to Ch. "Consequences Resulting from the Mystery of Subjectivity", p. 5.

The Good—according to the Augustinian formula—tends essentially to impart itself: Augustine (354-430), Bishop of the North African city of Hippo and the greatest of the Western Fathers, expressed the principle of *bonum diffusivum sui*, or the "diffusion of the Good", in his renowned formula, "Because God is good we exist" (*De doctrina christiana*, 1.31).

32: *Relativity in divinis* is an expression used by the author to refer to the prefiguration of the relative in the Absolute, without which no relationship between the two orders of the Absolute and the relative would either be possible or conceivable.

33: For the Latin phrase *credo ut intelligam* and its use by Anselm, see editor's note for Ch. "Aspects of the Theophanic Phenomenon of Consciousness", p. 15.

36: The Angelical Salutation—otherwise known as the *Ave Maria* or "Hail Mary"—describes the *Virgin* Mary as *gratia plena*, "full of grace" (cf. Luke 1:28, 42).

The third of the Ecumenical Councils, meeting in Ephesus (431), declared that the *Virgin* Mary is rightly called *Mater Dei* or "Mother of God".

The Problem of Possibility

41: Note 3: *The ambiguity of the semi-divine demiurge* refers to mythological figures, such as Iktomi the Spider among the Lakota and Leuk the Hare in North Africa, who are instrumental in carrying out the creation of the cosmos in an amoral and burlesque way. The author discusses the subject in greater detail in the chapter "The Demiurge in North American Mythology", in *Logic and Transcendence: A New Translation with Selected Letters*, ed. James S. Cutsinger (Bloomington, IN: World Wisdom, 2009).

42: Note 5: *The term "Being" does not necessarily have this restrictive meaning* [*God as Creator*] *since it can embrace both aspects in question* [*Beyond-Being* and *Being*] *and change its meaning or scope depending on the accompanying adjective or the context*: See below p. 45, Note 9, where the author specifies that terms such as *Esse* ("Being" in Latin) or *Allāh* ("God" in Arabic), can refer—in Christianity and Islam respectively—to both *Beyond-Being* and *Being*.

45: Note 8: *Lao Tzu* (sixth century B.C.) is the founder of Taoism and author of the *Tao Te Ching* ("The Book of the Way and Its Virtue").

Note 9: *Thomas* Aquinas (c. 1225-74), a giant among the medieval scholastics and author of the monumental *Summa Theologica*, is considered by the Roman Catholic Church to be the greatest Christian theologian in history.

46: *Asharites* are the disciples and continuators of the theology of al-Ashari (see editor's note for Ch. "Transcendence Is Not Contrary to Sense", p. 19, Note 4), who envisage God in exclusively anthropomorphic and voluntaristic terms.

In his *Fusūs al-Hikam*, or "Bezels of Wisdom", devoted to the wisdom of prophets, Muhyi ad-Din *Ibn Arabi* (see editor's note for Ch. "Aspects of the Theophanic Phenomenon of Consciousness", p. 12, Note 4) presents a criticism of Asharite theology in the *chapter on Seth*.

"*Had He willed, He would have guided all men*" (*Sūrah* "Thunder" [13]:31).

47: *The "fall of the angels"* is a predominantly Judeo-Christian and Islamic concept according to which God cast out certain angels, such as Lucifer or Iblis, who disobeyed His orders and rebelled against Him (cf. Is. 14:12-15; *Sūrah* "The Cow" [2]:34).

According to Ibn Arabi—still in the Fusūs—"*a possibility is that which can either be actualized or not actualized; but, in reality, the effective solution of this alternative is implied already in what this possibility represents in its state of principial immutability"* (chapter on Abraham).

48: "But Jesus beheld them, and said unto them, With men this is impossible; but *with God all things are possible"* (Matt. 19:26).

Structure and Universality of the Conditions of Existence

51: *The immediate point of departure of the sensible world was a unique sphere made of ether, or a "cloud", as diverse traditions express it.* For example, the Hindu *ākāsha*, the ancient Greek *aither*, and medieval alchemical *quinta essentia* were considered to be the subtle essence of all material forms, while in Islam the Prophet was asked, "Where did our Lord come to be before He created the creatures?" He replied, "He came to be in a *cloud*, neither above which nor below which was any air."

52: Note 2: The *Peripatetic* school of philosophy was founded by Aristotle (see editor's note for Ch. "Transcendence is Not Contrary to Sense, p. 20) in Athens in c. 335 B.C.; the name of the school is said to derive from the columns (*peripatoi*) of the Lyceum, where the Greek philosopher met with his disciples.

The *Peripatetic "categories"* were enumerated by Aristotle in his *Organon*, a collection of six works on logic, where they are defined either as the subject or predicate of a given logical proposition.

53: Note 4: *The medieval controversies between Nominalists and Realists.* The author remarks elsewhere that "In the medieval controversy of universals, the Nominalists were not wrong in looking on general ideas as abstractions or points of reference for thought, because from the point of view of reason they do indeed play this role; they were wrong, however, in blaming the Realists for seeing concrete realities in universals since from the standpoint of their intrinsic nature general qualities coincide no less really with the [Platonic] 'ideas' or principial roots of things" (*Logic and Transcendence: A New Translation with Selected Letters*, ed. James S. Cutsinger [Bloomington, IN: World Wisdom, 2009], p. 16).

54: Note 6: In its most representative form, *the Hindu doctrine of cosmic cycles* divides time *qualitatively* into *mahāyugas* or "great ages", each comprising four lesser ages (*yugas*) or periods of time, namely, the *Krita-Yuga* (the "golden" age of Western tradition), *Tretā-Yuga* ("silver"), *Dvāpara-Yuga* ("bronze"), and *Kali-Yuga* ("iron"). One *kalpa*, or "day of Brahmā", equals one thousand *mahāyugas*.

56: "And Jesus said unto him, No man, having put *his hand to the plough*, and looking back, *is fit for the Kingdom of God*" (Luke 9:62).

"Jesus said unto him, *Let the dead bury their dead*: but go thou and preach the kingdom of God" (Luke 9:60).

57: *Adequation constitutes the sufficient reason for the intelligence*: The author alludes here to the Scholastic definition of truth as the "adequation of reality and intellect" (*adaequatio rei et intellectus*).

Pythagoras of Samos (c. 569-c. 475), one of the greatest sages of ancient Greece, proclaimed a doctrine that was at once philosophical, mathematical, astronomical, and musical, teaching that numbers are not primarily quantitative realities but metaphysical and cosmological principles.

58: In Hindu cosmological doctrine, the "*days and nights of Brahmā*" refer to successive cycles of the manifestation and dissolution of the universe.

59: Note 12: *The Sufis, in conformity moreover with Koranic language, term spiritual concentration "remembrance of God"*: "Recite that which hath been inspired in thee of the Scripture, and establish worship. Lo! worship preserveth from lewdness and iniquity, but verily remembrance of God (*dhikr Allāh*) is greatest" (*Sūrah* "The Spider" [29]:45).

The Sufi mystic is called *ibn al-waqt* or "*son of the Moment*" inasmuch as he surrenders to the will of God in each and every present moment.

The symbolism of the frontal eye refers, in Hinduism and Buddhism, to the "third eye" or the sense of eternity, whose temporal reflection is the present moment.

Note 13: *Hesychasts* are monks of the Eastern Christian tradition whose aim is to attain to a state of *hesychia* or inner quietude through practice of the Jesus Prayer or other "prayer of the heart".

"*Keeping the spirit within the confines of the body*": John Climacus (c. 570-649), a monk and later abbot of Sinai, refers to the Hesychast as "one who seeks to circumscribe the incorporeal in his body" (*Ladder of Divine Ascent*).

60: *Shiva*, the third god of the Hindu trinity—Brahmā being the first and Vishnu the second—is associated with the powers of generation and destruction. His cosmic *dance*, the *Tāndava*, takes its name from his helper, Tandu, who taught the art of dance to the sage Bharata. These teachings were later codified in the *Natya Shastra*, from which the classical Bharata Natyam dance of India derives.

By virtue of his theomorphism: "And God said, Let us make man in our image, after our likeness" (Gen. 1:26).

62: "*The soul is all that which it knows*" is the doctrine of *Aristotle*, for whom "the thinking part of the soul, while impassible, must be capable of receiving the form of an object; that is, it must be potentially identical in character with its object without being the object" (*On the Soul*, 3.4).

Outline of a Spiritual Anthrology

65-66: "*Let us make man in our image, after our likeness*" (Gen. 1:27).

68: "He that loveth not knoweth not God; for *God is love*" (1 John 4:8).

69: *Mental formulation contributes to the actualization and assimilation of the immanent lights of the heart, and therein lies moreover the role of meditation:* Elsewhere the author remarks: "Reasoning can play no other part in knowledge than that of being the occasional cause of intellection, which arises suddenly—not continuously or progressively—as soon as the mental operation, conditioned in its turn by an intellectual intuition, possesses the quality that makes it a pure symbol" (*Spiritual Perspectives and Human Facts: A New Translation with Selected Letters*, ed. James S. Cutsinger [Bloomington, IN: World Wisdom, 2007], p. 7); "Reason has its rights: it can help to actualize a virtual intellection and then express an effective intellection" (*Logic and Transcendence: A New Translation with Selected Letters*, ed. James S. Cutsinger [Bloomington, IN: World Wisdom, 2009], p. 246).

71: *Piety is "supernaturally natural" to man:* The author makes use of this paradoxical expression to refer to the principle that "what is human is what is natural to man, and what is most essentially or most specifically natural to man is that which relates to the Absolute" (p. 6) or the supernatural.

73: *The hierarchy of mental types: the contemplative or sacerdotal, the combative or princely, the practical or industrious, the obedient or loyal:* These correspond to the fundamental caste (*varna*) types of Hinduism: the *brāhmana* (priest), *kshatriya* (warrior), *vaishya* (merchant, peasant, craftsman), and *shūdra* (laborer). See the author's *Castes and Races* (Bedfont: Perennial Books, 1982) for a more detailed treatment of this subject.

Note 5: *Men are differentiated by sex, age, temperament, zodiacal type, caste, and race:* See the author's chapter "Survey of Integral Anthropology", in *To Have a Center* (Bloomington, IN: World Wisdom, 1990), for a fuller treatment of this subject.

The Message of the Human Body

75: "*Made in the image of God*": "God created man in His own image, in the image of God created He him; male and female created He them" (Gen. 1:27).

The primordial androgyne—which is divided in two well before the successive entry of its halves into matter. Elsewhere the author remarks: "Our empirical matter, with all it comprises, is derived from a suprasensory and eminently plastic proto-matter; it is in this proto-matter that the primordial terrestrial being is reflected and 'incarnated', which is expressed in Hinduism in the myth of the sacrifice of *Purusha.* . . . In this proto-material *hyle* occurred the creation of the species and of man, a creation resembling the 'sudden crystallization of a supersaturated chemical solution'; after the 'creation of Eve'—the bipolarization of the primordial 'androgyne'—there occurred the 'fall', namely, the 'exteriorization' of the human couple, which brought in its train—since in the subtle and luminous proto-matter everything was bound together and interdependent—the exteriorization or 'materialization' of all other earthly creatures, hence their 'crystallization' in sensible, heavy, opaque, and mortal matter" (*Light on the Ancient Worlds: A New Translation with Selected Letters*, ed. Deborah Casey [Bloomington, IN: World Wisdom, 2006], pp. 35-36).

76: Note 2: "There appeared a *chariot of fire*, and horses of fire, and parted them both asunder; and *Elias* went up by a whirlwind into heaven" (2 Kings 2:11).

"And when he had spoken these things, while they beheld, he [Christ] was taken up; and a *cloud* received him out of their sight" (Acts 1:9).

77: *The* "*misogyny*" *of Buddhism* is evident in the early discourses and debates concerning the disputed ability of women to *attain Deliverance* and the requirement that *she must first be reborn in a masculine body.* "It is impossible that a woman should be the perfect rightfully Enlightened One. It is possible that a man should be the perfect rightfully Enlightened One" (*Majjhima Nikāya*, III 2.5). This "*misogyny*" is also evident in the disputes about the legitimacy of a female monastic order.

77-78: *Amidism* or *the Amidist way* of the Buddhist Pure Land (*Jōdo*) sect places strong emphasis on "*power of the Other*" (*tariki*), that is, attaining salvation through the *Mercy* of Amida Buddha, rather than on "*power of oneself*" (*jiriki*) through meditational practices.

78: *Lalla Yogishwari* was a fourteenth century Kashmiri poetess and saint;

among the gems of her poetry often quoted by the author are the lines: "My guru spake to me but one precept. He said unto me, 'From without enter thou the inmost part.' That to me became a rule and a precept, and therefore naked began I to dance."

Note 6: *The Brihadāranyaka Upanishad* is one of the most celebrated and authoritative sacred texts of Hinduism and relates the story of how *Maitreyi* became the wife of the sage *Yajnavalkya* out of a desire for his spiritual teaching. It contains the famous verse: "Verily it is not for the love of the spouse that the spouse is dear but for love of the Self" (2.4.5).

Apala, Visvavara, Sikata, Ghoda, and Lopmudra are among the women sages honored by Hindu tradition as ancient seers of the *Veda*s.

The *Yoga Vasishtha*, attributed to the sage Valmiki, is an Advaitic dialogue between a human spiritual master, Vasishtha, and his divine disciple, Rama, concerning the relationship between consciousness and Reality. It contains the story of prince *Shikhidhwaja*, who while hunting in the forest, happened upon the maiden *Chudala* and, overcome by her beauty and intelligence, promptly made her his wife, though it was not until many years later, having conquered the kingdom but being unable to conquer his mind, that he discovered she was a fully realized *jīvan-mukta*, utterly indifferent to the wealth and worldly power he had wished to bestow on her, and that she alone could be his *guru*.

80: *The seal of Solomon* is comprised of two superimposed equilateral triangles, one with its apex pointing upward, and the other with its apex pointing downward.

81: Note 14: The Roman historian Publius Cornelius *Tacitus* (c. 55-c. 117) wrote an ethnographic study of the *Germanic tribes* entitled *De Origine et situ Germanorum* ("The Origin and Location of the Germans"), in which he contrasted their simplicity with the sophistication of Rome.

84: *The refusal of Lucifer to bow down before Adam*: "And when We [God] said unto the angels: Prostrate yourselves before Adam, they fell prostrate, all save Iblis. He demurred through pride, and so became a disbeliever" (*Sūrah* "The Cow" [2]:34); "He [God] said: What hindered thee that thou didst not fall prostrate when I bade thee? (Iblis) said: I am better than him. Thou createdst me of fire while him Thou didst create of mud" (*Sūrah* "The Heights" [7]:12).

The *Rāmāyana*, a Hindu epic tale attributed to the sage Valmiki, recounts the story of Rama, the seventh *Avatāra* of Vishnu. In Rama's battle against the demon king Ravana for possession of his abducted wife, Sita, he is aided by Hanuman, king of the *apes*.

Note 19: On the "*silver age*" (*Tretā-Yuga*) and "*iron age*" (*Kali-Yuga*) see editor's note for Ch. "Structure and Universality of the Conditions of Existence", p. 54, Note 6.

Note 21: *What monotheistc symbolism calls the "fall of Adam"*: "And unto Adam he [God] said, Because thou hast hearkened unto the voice of thy wife, and hast eaten of the tree, of which I commanded thee, saying, Thou shalt not eat of it: cursed is the ground for thy sake; in sorrow shalt thou eat of it all the days of thy life; Thorns also and thistles shall it bring forth to thee; and thou shalt eat the herb of the field; In the sweat of thy face shalt thou eat bread, till thou return unto the ground; for out of it wast thou taken: for dust thou art, and unto dust shalt thou return" (Gen. 3:17-19).

"*The resurrection of the flesh*": "If the dead are not raised, then Christ has not been raised. If Christ has not been raised, your faith is futile and you are still in your sins. Then those also who have fallen asleep in Christ have perished" (1 Cor. 15:13-18).

85: *Buddhism, as we already noted, is essentially a masculine, abstract, negative, ascetic, and heroic spirituality*: "One indeed is one's own refuge; how can others be a refuge to one? With oneself thoroughly tamed, one can attain a refuge . . . , which is so difficult to attain" (*Dhammapada*, 160); "You yourselves should make the effort; the *Tathāgatas* (Buddhas) only can show the way. Those who practice the tranquillity and insight meditation are freed from the bond of [the demon] Mara" (*Dhammapada*, 276).

86: Note 22: *In Krishnaism, the masculine adepts consider themselves as gopīs, lovers of Krishna*: Hindu tradition tells of the youthful dalliance of the *Avatāra* Krishna with the adoring *gopīs* or cowherd girls of Vrindavan.

The Sense of the Sacred

87: The "*Motionless Mover*", or Unmoved Mover, is Aristotle's (see editor's note for Ch. "Transcendence is Not Contrary to Sense", p. 20) classic expression for the divine Principle, as in the *Metaphysics*, 1072b.

87-88: Note 2: The term "*pantheism*" is closely associated with the Dutch philosopher Baruch Spinoza (1632-77), whose formula *Deus sive Natura*, "God or Nature", amounted to equating the Divine with nature, thereby negating the *transcendence* of God.

89: *Ceremonies often form the framework of rites*: "A rite is an action the very form of which is the result of a Divine Revelation. Thus the perpetuation of a rite is itself a mode of Revelation, and Revelation is present in the rite in both its aspects—the intellectual and the ontological" (Titus Burckhardt, *Introduction to Sufi Doctrine* [Bloomington, IN: World Wisdom, 2008], p. 89); "Now, it might be asked why ceremonies are thus attached to rites, as if the 'non-human' had need of this human assistance, when it should much rather remain as far removed as possible from such contingencies. The answer is that all of this is simply a consequence of the need to take into account the actual conditions of terrestrial humanity, at least in this or that period of its existence; it is a concession made to what is, from the spiritual point of view, a certain state of degeneration on the part of the men who are called to participate in the rites, for it is they and not the rites who need the help of ceremonies" (René Guénon, *Perspectives on Initiation* [Hillsdale, NY: Sophia Perennis, 2001], p. 133).

90: "*Platonic recollection*" refers to the doctrine, notably presented in the dialogues *Phaedo* and *Meno*, according to which real knowledge is inscribed in human intelligence from eternity and needs merely to be "recollected" (*anamnesis*) through intellectual intuition.

Basil the Great (c. 330-379), the Greek bishop of Caesaria and one of the Cappadocian Fathers, was instrumental in the codification and elaboration of early Christian liturgy, on which he remarks: "We are not content in the liturgy simply to recite the words recorded by St. Paul or the Gospels, but *we add others before and after to lend greater power to the mysteries.* We have received these words from unwritten teachings . . . which our fathers guarded in silence, safe from meddling and petty curiosity" (*On the Holy Spirit*, 27:65-66).

In Eastern Orthodox churches *iconostases* are screens of icons that separate the nave from the sanctuary.

In Western churches *golden retables* are ornamental screenlike structures placed behind the altar.

92: *David was the last to want to be king, but it is he who was chosen*: "Again, Jesse made seven of his sons to pass before Samuel. And Samuel said unto Jesse, The Lord hath not chosen these. And Samuel said unto Jesse, Are here all thy children? And he said, There remaineth yet the youngest, and, behold, he keepeth the sheep. And Samuel said unto Jesse, Send and fetch him: for we will not sit down till he come hither. And he sent, and brought him in. Now he was ruddy, and withal of a beautiful countenance, and goodly to look to. And the Lord said, Arise, anoint him: for this is he" (1 Sam. 16:10-12).

Plotinus (c. 205-270), founder of the Neoplatonic school, endeavored to synthesize the teachings of Plato and Aristotle in his monumental *Enneads.* The second Tractate of the first *Ennead* is entitled "On Virtue" and deals with the subject of the acquisition of the *moral qualities* by the *metaphysician* or philosopher.

94: *If "God exists"—really and fully, and not as some unconscious and passive "power" as the naturalists and deists would have it:* While naturalists reduce all phenomena to the status of products of the laws of nature, deists reject revelation and religion in asserting that only human reason and natural law are sufficient to establish the existence of a supreme Being.

96: Note 7: *Men cry out, faint, fall into ecstasy, sometimes die, under the effect of a given manifestation of* barakah, *sometimes even following a particularly enlightening or striking formulation:* "Bahram recited the attestation, 'I bear witness that there is no god but God, and I bear witness that Muhammad is the Apostle of God.' Thereupon Ahmad cried aloud and fainted. . . . Whenever Sahl partook in a mystic audition he went into ecstasy and would continue rapt for five days, eating no food" (Farid ad-Din Attar, *Muslim Saints and Mystics*).

Note 8: The *Biblical stories up to and including that of the Tower of Babel* are found in the Book of Genesis 1-11.

To Refuse or To Accept Revelation

99: *Many Koranic stories present to us, with even more insistence than the Bible, the following motif: the prophets preach and the people reject the Message; God punishes them for this rejection; and He rewards those men who believe:* "And Lot! (Remember) when he said unto his folk: Will ye commit abomination such as no creature ever did before you? Lo! ye come with lust unto men instead of women. Nay, but ye are wanton folk. And the answer of his people was only that they said (one to another): Turn them out of your township. They are folk, forsooth, who keep pure. And We rescued him and his household, save his wife, who was of those who stayed behind. And We rained a rain upon them. See now the nature of the consequence of evil-doers!" (*Sūrah* "The Heights" [7]:80-84); "And lo! Elias was of those sent (to warn), When he said unto his folk: Will ye not ward off (evil)? Will ye cry unto Baal and forsake the best of creators, God, your Lord and Lord of your forefathers? But they denied him, so they surely will be haled forth (to the doom). Save single minded slaves of God. And we left for him among the later folk (the salutation): Peace be unto Elias! Lo! thus do We reward the good. Lo! he is one of our believing slaves" (*Sūrah* "Ranged in Rows" [37]:123-132), *passim.*

The *Pharisees* were a powerful Jewish religious school at the time of Jesus that laid emphasis on outer actions and legal conformity in a spirit of self-righteous formalism.

The pagan Arabs were the polytheistic inhabitants of the Arabian Peninsula before and during the time of the Prophet Muhammad.

100: *Pythagorean initiates* were followers of the esoteric mysteries established by Pythagoras (see editor's note for Ch. "Structure and Universality of the Conditions of Existence", p. 57).

Note 2: *Numerous passages in the Koran likewise point out that the Arabs believed neither in the immortality of the soul nor in resurrection, whereas their ancestors did believe in them*: "And they say: lo! this is mere magic; When we are dead and have become dust and bones, shall we then, forsooth, be raised (again)? And our forefathers?" (*Sūrah* "Ranged in Rows" [37]:15-17); "And the disbelievers say: This is a strange thing: When we are dead and have become dust (shall we be brought back again)? That would be a far return!" (*Sūrah* "Qaf" [50]:2-3), *passim.*

Note 3: "But when Jesus heard that, he said unto them, *They that are whole need not a physician,* but they that are sick" (Matt. 9:12).

Go ye therefore, and teach all nations, baptizing them in the name of the Father, and of the Son, and of the Holy Ghost" (Matt. 28:19).

101: The Spanish and Portuguese *conquistadores* were soldiers, explorers, and adventurers who conquered parts of South America in the fifteenth to seventeenth centuries on behalf of the Spanish Empire and Portuguese Empire; in their conquests they killed many of the native *Indians of Peru and Mexico.*

Note 4: *The Sermon on the Mount* is recorded in the Gospel of Matthew (Chaps. 5-7) and contains the following *discourse* on the Beatitudes: "Blessed are the poor in spirit: for theirs is the kingdom of heaven. Blessed are they that mourn: for they shall be comforted. Blessed are the meek: for they shall inherit the earth. Blessed are they which do hunger and thirst after righteousness: for they shall be filled. Blessed are the merciful: for they shall obtain mercy. Blessed are the pure in heart: for they shall see God. Blessed are the peacemakers: for they shall be called the children of God. Blessed are they which are persecuted for righteousness' sake: for theirs is the kingdom of heaven" (Matt. 5:3-10).

Note 5: The author's *chapter "La Marge humaine"*, from his *book, Forme et Substance dans les Religions* (Paris: Dervy Livres, 1975), appeared in English as "The Human Margin", in *Form and Substance in the Religions* (Bloomington, IN: World Wisdom, 2002).

Note 6: *Which led Jesus to speak of "human prescriptions" even though they were "traditional"*: "But in vain they do worship me, teaching for doctrines the commandments of men" (Matt. 15:9; Mark 7:7).

102: The Christian *Sacraments* are divinely instituted rites and means of grace, comprising Baptism, Confirmation, Penance, the Eucharist, Matrimony, Holy Orders, and Extreme Unction.

The *Sadducees* were a heterodox Jewish religious sect *culled largely from among the priests and aristocrats*, who maintained the Temple of Jerusalem at the time of Jesus.

The *Torah* (literally, "instruction, teaching") is the written law of God, as revealed to Moses on Sinai and embodied in the Pentateuch (Genesis, Exodus, Leviticus, Numbers, Deuteronomy).

The *Mishnah* (literally "repetition") is a collection of Jewish oral tradition, including commentary on the *Torah* and an application of its principles, which is said to have been given to Moses, but which was only made known to the spiritual and temporal authorities of the tradition, the Sanhedrin, by Moses' successor, the prophet Joshua; it is also referred to as the oral *Torah.*

Note 7: *The Babylonian captivity* refers to a period of Jewish deportation and exile in Babylon, following the destruction of the First Temple of Jerusalem in the sixth century B.C.

103: Note 11: "Why do thy *disciples* transgress the tradition of the elders? for they *wash not* their *hands* when they eat bread" (Matt. 15:2).

104: The *Essenes* (the "holy, pious ones") were an ancient Jewish ascetical sect, known for their communitarian life and emphasis on celibacy and simplicity. The author relates them to the *Cabalists*—Jewish mystics who flourished in medieval Europe and Palestine—on account of their esoteric and contemplative leanings.

The *Talmud* (literally, "learning, study") is a body of Jewish rabbinical writings and traditional commentaries based on the oral law given to Moses on

Sinai. It claims that "Jesus the Nazarene . . . practiced sorcery and instigated and seduced Israel to idolatry" (Sanhedrin, 43a).

105: *The Buddha rejected the* Veda: Elsewhere the author explains the reasons for this rejection in greater detail: "The arguments of Christianity and Buddhism with regard to the traditional forms from which they may be said to have respectively issued, namely Judaism in the first case and Hinduism in the second . . . are symbolically true, in the sense that the rejected forms are not considered in themselves and from the standpoint of their intrinsic truth, but solely in certain contingent and negative aspects that are due to a partial decadence; the rejection of the *Veda* therefore corresponds to a truth in so far as this scripture is viewed exclusively as the symbol of a sterile erudition which was highly developed and widespread in the time of Buddha, and the rejection by St. Paul of the Jewish Law was justified in so far as the latter corresponded to a Pharisaical formalism lacking spiritual life. If a new Revelation may thus justifiably depreciate traditional values of an earlier origin, it is because it is independent of these values and has no need of them, since it possesses equivalent values of its own and is therefore entirely self-sufficient" (*The Transcendent Unity of Religions* [Wheaton, IL: Quest, 1984], pp. 95-96).

Note 13: *The excessively unilateral interpretation of the "Old Law", as well as the misinterpretation of sexuality, derive from the Epistles and not from the Gospel*: "Christ hath redeemed us from the curse of the law" (Gal. 3:13); "For sin shall not have dominion over you: for ye are not under the law, but under grace" (Rom. 6:14); "For the letter killeth, but the spirit giveth life" (2 Cor. 3:6); "It is good for a man not to touch a woman. Nevertheless, to avoid fornication, let every man have his own wife, and let every woman have her own husband. . . . I say therefore to the unmarried and widows, it is good for them if they abide even as I [celibate]. But if they cannot contain, let them marry: for it is better to marry than to burn" (1 Cor. 7:1-2, 8-9).

Note 14: *The intervention of the Paraclete*: "And I will pray the Father, and he shall give you another Comforter, that he may abide with you for ever; . . . But the Comforter, which is the Holy Ghost, whom the Father will send in my name, he shall teach you all things, and bring all things to your remembrance, whatsoever I have said unto you" (John 14:16, 26).

106: *The vicar of Saint Peter* is the pope, or successor of the apostle Peter, who was the first pope of the Church.

Note 15: *The words of Christ to Peter near the Lake of Tiberias*: "I say also unto thee, That thou art Peter, and upon this rock I will build my church; and the gates of hell shall not prevail against it. And I will give unto thee the keys of the kingdom of heaven: and whatsoever thou shalt bind on earth shall be bound in heaven, and whatsoever thou shalt loose on earth shall be loosed in heaven" (Matt. 16:18-19).

The *three denials* of the apostle *Peter* are related in Matthew 26:69-75, Mark 14:66-72, Luke 22:54-62, and John 18:25-27.

The retro Satanas *which Christ hurled at Peter on the threshold of the Passion*: "From that time forth began Jesus to shew unto his disciples, how that he must go unto Jerusalem, and suffer many things of the elders and chief priests and scribes, and be killed, and be raised again the third day. Then Peter took him, and began to rebuke him, saying, Be it far from thee, Lord: this shall not be unto thee. But he turned, and said unto Peter, Get thee behind me, Satan: thou art an offence unto me: for thou savourest not the things that be of God, but those that be of men. Then said Jesus unto his disciples, If any man will come after me, let him deny himself, and take up his cross, and follow me" (Matt. 16:21-24).

The "beloved disciple" and adopted son of Mary was John: "Now there was leaning on Jesus' bosom one of his disciples, whom Jesus loved" (John 13:23); "When Jesus therefore saw his mother, and the disciple standing by, whom he loved, he saith unto his mother, Woman, behold thy son!" (John 1:26).

107: For *Neoplatonism* see editor's note for Ch. "The Sense of the Sacred", p. 92.

For *Aristotelianism* see editor's note for Ch. "Transcendence is Not Contrary to Sense", p. 20 and Ch. "Structure and Universality of the Conditions of Existence", p. 52, Note 2.

Aristotle (see editor's note for Ch. "Transcendence is Not Contrary to Sense, p. 20) is known as the *Stagirite* because he was born in the Ionian city of Stagira in Chalcidice.

Note 17: *Stoicism* was a school of Hellenistic philosophy founded by Zeno of Citium (c. 334-c. 262 B.C.) in Athens in the third century B.C. Among its later adherents were Seneca (c. 4 B.C.-65 A.D.), Epictetus (55-135 A.D.), and Emperor Marcus Aurelius (121-180 A.D.). The author remarks that its *ambiguity* stems from "its pantheistic immanentism [which] can be viewed as an intentionally fragmentary perspective exclusively aimed at a heroic morality, or as a heterodoxy pure and simple" ("The Perennial Philosophy", in *The Unanimous Tradition: Essays on the Essential Unity of All Religions*, ed. Ranjit Fernando [Colombo: Sri Lanka Institute of Traditional Studies, 1991], p. 23n).

108: "And Jacob said unto his father, *I am Esau* thy firstborn; I have done according as thou badest me: arise, I pray thee, sit and eat of my venison, that thy soul may bless me" (Gen. 27:19).

109: "And *Cain knew his wife,* and she conceived, and bare Enoch: and he builded a city, and called the name of the city, after the name of his son, Enoch" (Gen. 4:17).

Note 18: *Abu Bakr* (d. 634), one of the Prophet Muhammad's foremost Companions and the first caliph of Islam, denied the Prophet's daughter *Fatimah the right to her inheritance* of the Oasis of Fadak *for legal reasons.*

Note 19: The Sefer ha-*Zohar,* that is, "The Book of Splendor", published in Spain c. 1285, is an esoteric commentary on the *Torah* and the most important text in the Jewish mystical tradition of Cabalah.

Note 20: "For it came to pass, when *Solomon* was old, that his *wives* turned away his heart after other gods: and his heart was not perfect with the Lord his God, as was the heart of David his father. For Solomon went after Ashtoreth the goddess of the Zidonians, and after Milcom the abomination of the Ammonites. And Solomon did evil in the sight of the Lord, and went not fully after the Lord, as did David his father. Then did Solomon build an high place for Chemosh, the abomination of Moab, in the hill that is before Jerusalem, and for Molech, the abomination of the children of Ammon. And likewise did he for all his strange wives, which burnt incense and sacrificed unto their gods" (1 Kings 11:4-10).

"And Solomon *slept with his fathers,* and was buried in the city of David his father: and Rehoboam his son reigned in his stead" (1 Kings 11:43).

111: Quintus Septimius Florens *Tertullian* (c. 160-c. 225) was an early Christian apologist and ascetical writer whose treatise *De Carne Christi* ("On the Flesh of Christ") says of the death of the Son of God that it is *credibile quia ineptum est,* that is, "believable because it is unsuitable" (5:4).

Note 26: The Latin phrase *credo quia absurdum* means, "I believe because it is absurd."

The Shinto commentator Motoori Norinaga (1730-1801), a scholar of the Edo period, advocated the spirit and values of the indigenous Japanese Shinto religion against what he considered to be the negative influence of Confucianism.

112: *It is the Logos who shines in the darkness; who at first is uncomprehended* *and who then triumphs*: "And the light shineth in darkness; and the darkness comprehended it not" (John 1:5).

113: Note 27: *Gamaliel*, a teacher of Saint Paul (Acts 22:3), advised his fellow members of the Sanhedrin not to put Peter and the other Apostles to death, using the *argument* that "if this counsel or this work be of men, it will come to nought: but if it be of God, ye cannot overthrow it" (Acts 5:38-39).

Note 28: Louis *Massignon* (1883-1962), a foremost French Islamicist best known for his magisterial study of the Sufi saint Mansur al-Hallaj, considered Muslims as spiritual heirs to Abraham, and advocated a spiritual "de-centering" as a necessary precondition for understanding other faiths.

114: *We are as far as can be from approving a gratuitous and sentimentalist "ecumenism"*: Elsewhere the author has remarked: "I am completely against ecumenism as it is practiced today—with its ineffective 'dialogues' and gratuitous and sentimental gestures amounting to nothing. Certainly an understanding between religions is possible and even necessary, though solely on the basis of common ideas and common interests and not on the dogmatic plane. The common ideas are a transcendent, perfect, all-powerful, merciful Absolute, then a hereafter that is either good or bad depending on our merits or demerits; all the religions, including Buddhism—Buddhist 'atheism' is simply a misunderstanding—are in agreement on these points. The common interests are a defense against materialism, atheism, perversion, subversion, and modernism in all its guises. I believe Pius XII once said that the wars between Christians and Muslims were but domestic quarrels compared to the present opposition between the world of the religions and that of militant materialism-atheism; he also said it was a consolation to know that there are millions of men who prostrate themselves five times a day before God" (*Splendor of the True: A Frithjof Schuon Reader*, ed. James S. Cutsinger [Albany, NY: State University of New York Press, 2013], p. 220).

Note 28 (cont.): *The Shinto divinities became Bodhisattvas, sometimes through their own intervention, in dreams or visions or by way of oracles*: The author comments further: "The Asiatic religions—Hinduism, Buddhism, Taoism—because of their spiritual transparency—absorb foreign traditional elements quite readily; so much so that a Shintoist divinity becomes a *Bodhisattva* without altering its essence, since the respective names cover universal realities." A translator's note adds: "It is recorded of the Emperor Shomu that in the year 742 A.D. he sent an envoy to the [Shintoist] Ise shrine, symbolical center for the nation of Japan, to request an oracle from the Sun Goddess [Amaterasu] concerning his projected building of the great Buddhist temple Todaiji at Nara; a favorable oracle was granted. Soon after that the Emperor had a dream in which the Goddess herself appeared to him saying, 'This is the land of the Gods, the people should revere them. In my essence I am the (solar) Buddha Vairochana. Let my people understand this and take refuge in the Law of the Buddhas'" (*Treasures of Buddhism* [Bloomington, IN: World Wisdom, 1993], p. 169).

Note 29: *There is "no salvation outside the Church"*, or *extra ecclesiam nulla salus*, is a fundamental dogma of the Christian faith.

121: Note 30: By the *dreamers of the eighteenth century* the author refers particularly to the rationalist philosophers of the Enlightenment, such as Voltaire (1694-1778), Diderot (1713-1784), and D'Alembert (1717-1783), whose *ancient civism and freemasonic idealism* sought to undermine and eradicate the authority of the monarchy and the Church.

Note 31: The *Decalogue* refers to the Ten Commandments given by God to Moses on Mount Sinai (Exod. 20:1-17).

123: *The "social doctrines" of the Church* are a body of Catholic teachings on labor, economics, and the role of the state, whose main foundations are Leo XIII's encyclical letter *Rerum Novarum* (1891) and Pius XI's *Quadragesimo Anno* (1931), which reject socialism and *laissez-faire* liberalism.

Note 33: Cardinal *Richelieu* (1585-1642), the First Minister of King Louis XIII, *attacked* the rights and influence of the *guilds* in the name of political and economic centralization.

Note 34: Mohandas K. *Gandhi* (1869-1948) was the leader of the non-violent independence movement in British-ruled India. His message laid a strong emphasis on *religion* and the *crafts* in promoting individual and societal well-being. As a symbol of this he encouraged Indians to follow his *good example* in producing homespun cloth on the spinning wheel.

In nineteenth-century France, *the monarchist and traditional right-wing* was represented by the Legitimists—supporters of the eldest branch of the Bourbon family—who sought to uphold the alliance of the Throne and the Church and bring about the restoration of the *Ancien Régime*.

The ambiguous "right-wing" born in the nineteenth century in the shadow of the machine primarily refers to the Orléanists—so named because favorable to the cadet branch called the House of Orléans—who supported a constitutional monarchy and were associated with the advent of the industrial revolution in France.

124: The Russian novelist Leo *Tolstoy* (1828-1910) was author of renowned works such as *War and Peace* and *Anna Karenina*. In his short story, "The Coffee-House of Surat", one of *Tolstoy's characters* says: "All human temples are built on the model of this temple, which is God's own world. Every temple has its fonts, its vaulted roof, its lamps, its pictures or sculptures, its inscriptions, its books of the law, its offerings, its altars, and its priests. But in what temple is there such a *font as the ocean*; such a vault as that of the heavens; such lamps as the sun, moon, and stars; or any figures to be compared with living, loving, mutually-helpful men?"

125: The *Upanishads*, also referred to as the *Vedānta* since they were traditionally placed at the "end" of the *Vedas*, are Hindu scriptures which contain metaphysical, mystical, and esoteric doctrine.

The *Bhagavad Gītā*, the best known and arguably the most important of all Hindu sacred texts and part of the much longer epic *Mahābhārata*, consists of a dialogue between the prince Arjuna and his charioteer, the *Avatāra* Krishna, concerning the different paths to God.

"*He who has seen me (the Prophet) has seen God*" (*hadīth*).

"*God became man in order that man might become God*" is the formulation of Irenaeus (c. 130-c. 200) and Athanasius (*c.* 296-373), among other Church Fathers (see editor's note for Ch. "Transcendence Is Not Contrary to Sense", p. 23).

Note 37: *Honen Shonin* (1133-1212) was the founder of the Japanese school of *Jōdo* or Pure Land Buddhism, also known as the *Amidist tradition* (see editor's note for Ch. "The Message of the Human Body", p. 78).

126: The *Encyclopedists* were a group of Enlightenment philosophers and scientists who collaborated to produce the 28 volume French *Encyclopedia*, or *Systematic Dictionary of the Sciences, Arts, and Crafts* between 1751 and 1772.

128: For the Latin phrase *credo ut intelligam* and its use by Anselm, see editor's note for Ch. "Aspects of the Theophanic Phenomenon of Consciousness", p. 15.

129: Note 40: *Arianism* is an early Christian heresy, attributed to Arius (250-336), which considered the Son to be a created being, and therefore not substantially one with the Father.

Shiism is an Islamic sect that looks to Ali and his descendents as the legitimate and authoritative representatives of the Prophet Muhammad.

Selections from Letters and Other Previously Unpublished Writings

133: Selection 1: "The Two Churches", unpublished, c. 1950.

Selection 2: "Concerning *An Introduction to Christian Esoterism*", unpublished, c. 1980.

134: The *initiates of Eleusis* and *Samothrace* were affiliated to the ancient Greek mystery religions.

Selection 3: Letter of February 14, 1978.

135: *Meister Eckhart* (see editor's note for Ch. "Aspects of the Theophanic Phenomenon of Consciousness", p. 13) wrote *some extremely bold formulations about the distinction between "Being" and "Beyond-Being"* such as: "*God and Godhead* are as different as *earth* is from *Heaven*" (Sermon *Nolite timere eos...*).

Selection 4: Letter of January 13, 1957.

136: Selection 5: Letter of January 18, 1982.

Meister Eckhart indicates the sacredness of food and of eating and drinking in general when he remarks that "if someone were as well prepared for ordinary nourishment as he is for the holy sacrament [*the Eucharist*], he would receive God in this nourishment just as fully as in the sacrament itself" (quoted in *Christianity/Islam: Perspectives on Esoteric Ecumenism: A New Translation with Selected Letters*, ed. James S. Cutsinger [Bloomington, IN: World Wisdom, 2008], p. 21).

Selection 6: Letter of January, 23, 1983.

137: Selection 7: Letter of April 14, 1970.

Selection 8: Letter of February 15, 1974.

For *Krishna* see editor's note for Ch. "The Message of the Human Body", p. 86, Note 22.

138: For the *Fedeli d'Amore* see editor's note for Ch. "Aspects of the Theophanic Phenomenon of Consciousness", p. 12, Note 4.

Selection 9: "Concerning *An Introduction to Christian Esoterism*", unpublished, c. 1980.

On *Augustine* and *the innate tendency of the Good to impart itself* see editor's note for Ch. "The Interplay of the Hypostases", p. 31.

Note 1: Jean-Jacques *Olier* (1608-1657) was a French priest and the founder of the Society of Saint-Sulpice.

139: Selection 10: "Trinitarian Dogma and Metaphysical Truth", unpublished, c. 1950.

Note 2: *Divergences between Latins and Greeks:* One reason for the schism between Orthodoxy and Roman Catholicism was the unilateral decision of the West to interpolate the word *filioque* into the Latin text of the Nicene Creed, thus expressing a double procession of the Holy Spirit from the Father "and the Son".

John Damascene, or *John of Damascus* (c. 675-c. 749), was a Greek theologian and "doctor of the church", best known for his *Fount of Wisdom.*

140: In this instance the author uses the phrase *"the religious point of view"* to refer to the exoteric point of view in general.

141: Selection 11: Letter of February 3, 1978.

"Be ye therefore perfect, even as your Father which is in heaven is perfect" (Matt. 5:48).

142: Selection 12: "Concerning the Five Divine Presences and the Transcendent Unity of Religions", July 1992.

For *the sentences* referred to in the author's *From the Divine to the Human*, see Ch. "Transcendence is Not Contrary to Sense", pp. 23-24.

The Sufi *metaphysical doctrine* of the *Five Divine Presences* distinguishes five ontological degrees within the essential unity of the Real, ranging from the *impersonal Divinity* to the *personal God* to the *heavenly world* to *psychism* to *matter*. See the author's chapter "The Five Divine Presences", in *Form and Substance in the Religions* (Bloomington, IN: World Wisdom, 2002), for an extensive presentation of this subject.

The author's first French book, entitled *De l'Unité transcendante des religions* (Paris: Gallimard, 1948), appeared in English as *The Transcendent Unity of Religions* (London: Faber & Faber; New York: Pantheon, 1953). In its preface the author explains that "if the expression 'transcendent unity' is used, it means that the unity of the religious forms must be realized in a purely inward and spiritual way and without prejudice to any particular form" (Wheaton, IL: Quest Books, 1984, p. xxxiv).

142-43: For *Meister Eckhart's* distinction between *the personal God* (Gott)

175

and the impersonal *Godhead or Divinity* (Gottheit), see Ch. "Transcendence is Not Contrary to Sense", pp. 18-19, Note 3.

143: Selection 13: "Travel Meditations", *Studies in Comparative Religion*, Vol. 12, Nos. 1 & 2, Winter-Spring, 1978.

The Mystery of Numbers

145: "The Mystery of Numbers" was first published in French as "Le mystère des nombres", *Connaissance des Religions*, July-December, 1995; it first appeared in *The Eye of the Heart: Metaphysics, Cosmology, Spiritual Life* (Bloomington, IN: World Wisdom, 1997), an English edition of the author's *L'Œil du Cœur* (Paris: Gallimard, 1950; Paris: Dervy-Livres, 1974) under the title "Concerning Pythagorean Numbers".

For *Pythagoras* see editor's note for Ch. "Structure and Universality of the Conditions of Existence", p. 57.

Note 1: The *four Archangels* of *Islamic angelology* are Gabriel (Arabic: Jibrail), Michael (Mikhail), Raphael (Israfil), and Azrael (Izrail). See the author's chapter "*An-Nūr*" in *Dimensions of Islam* (London: George Allen & Unwin, 1969) for a more detailed treatment of this subject.

146: "And God said unto Moses, I am *that I am*" (Ex. 3:14).

147: Note 2: On *the Platonic "ideas"* as *celestial prototypes* see editor's note for Ch. "Transcendence Is Not Contrary to Sense", p. 25.

148: According to Meister Eckhart (see editor's note for Ch. "Aspects of the Theophanic Phenomenon of Consciousness", p. 13), "There is something in the soul that is uncreated and uncreatable" (*aliquid* est in anima quod est *increatum et increabile*), namely the *pure Intellect*.

"Behold, *the kingdom of God is within you*" (Luke 17:21).

"An invisible and subtle essence is the Spirit of the whole universe. That is Reality. That is Truth. *That art thou (Tat tvam asi)*" (*Chāndogya Upanishad*, 7.6).

150: "*I am black, but beautiful,* O ye daughters of Jerusalem, as the tents of Kedar, as the curtains of Solomon" (Song of Sol. 1:5).

"*Say: God is One; God is impenetrable; He begetteth not nor is He begotten; and there is none like unto Him*" (*Sūrah* "Purification" [112]:1-4).

GLOSSARY OF FOREIGN TERMS AND PHRASES

Ab intra (Latin): literally, "from within"; proceeding from something intrinsic or internal.

A contrario (Latin): literally "from the opposite"; a form of argument in which a position is established or strengthened by highlighting the deficiencies of what opposes it.

Ad alterum (Latin): literally, "toward another"; defined in relationship to something else; in contrast to *ad se*.

Ad infinitum (Latin): literally, "to infinity"; without end, forever.

Ad se (Latin): literally, "toward itself"; defined solely by or with respect to itself; in contrast to *ad alterum*.

Advaita (Sanskrit): "non-dualist" interpretation of the *Vedānta*; Hindu doctrine according to which the seeming multiplicity of things is regarded as the product of ignorance, the only true reality being *Brahma*, the One, the Absolute, the Infinite, which is the unchanging ground of appearance.

A fortiori (Latin): literally, "from greater reason"; used when drawing a conclusion inferred to be even stronger than the one already put forward.

Agathon (Greek): "the sovereign good"; in Platonism, a name for the First Principle or Supreme Reality.

Ānanda (Sanskrit): "bliss, beatitude, joy"; one of the three essential aspects of *Apara-Brahma*, together with *Sat*, "being", and *Chit*, "consciousness".

Anthropos (Greek): the human being, male or female.

Apara-Brahma (Sanskrit): the "non-supreme" or penultimate *Brahma*, also called *Brahma saguna*; in Schuon's teaching, the "relative Absolute".

A posteriori (Latin): literally, "from after"; proceeding from effect to cause or from experience to principle.

A priori (Latin): literally, "from before"; proceeding from cause to effect or from principle to experience.

'Ārif bi 'Llāh (Arabic): literally, "knower by God"; in Sufism, one who has

attained supreme spiritual knowledge, or *ma'rifah.*

Ātmā or *Ātman* (Sanskrit): the real or true "Self" underlying all things; in the perspective of *Advaita Vedānta*, identical with *Brahma.*

Avatāra (Sanskrit): a divine "descent"; the incarnation or manifestation of God, especially of Vishnu in the Hindu tradition.

Barakah (Arabic): "blessing", grace; in Islam, a spiritual influence or energy emanating originally from God, but often attached to sacred objects and spiritual persons.

Bhakti or *bhakti-mārga* (Sanskrit): the spiritual "path" (*mārga*) of "love" (*bhakti*) and devotion; see *jnāna* and *karma.*

Bodhi (Sanskrit and Pali): literally "enlightened, awakened"; in Buddhism, the supreme experience of enlightenment.

Bodhisattva (Sanskrit): literally, "enlightenment-being"; in *Theravāda* Buddhism, one who is on the way to enlightenment; in *Mahāyāna* Buddhism, one who postpones his own final enlightenment and entry into *Nirvāna* in order to aid all other sentient beings in their quest for Buddhahood.

Brahma or *Brahman* (Sanskrit): the Supreme Reality, the Absolute; see *apara-Brahma* and *para-Brahma.*

Chit (Sanskrit): "consciousness"; one of the three essential aspects of *Apara-Brahma,* together with *Sat,* "being", and *Ānanda,* "bliss, beatitude, joy".

Cogito ergo sum (Latin): "I think; therefore I am."

Corruptio optimi pessima (Latin): a scholastic axiom meaning, the "corruption of the best is the worst".

Creatio ex nihilo (Latin): literally "creation out of nothing"; a Semitic monotheistic dogma according to which God drew creation out of no pre-existent reality; often set in contrast to emanationist cosmogonies.

Credo ut intelligam (Latin): "I believe so that I may understand."

Dākinī (Sanskrit): in Tibetan Buddhism, a female deity who embodies the energy of enlightenment.

De facto (Latin): literally, "from the fact"; denoting something that exists "in fact", if not necessarily "by right".

De jure (Latin): literally, "by right"; an expression often used in contradistinction with *de facto*.

Deus absconditus (Latin): literally, "hidden God"; God as transcendent and hence inaccessible to human thought or perception.

Dhikru 'Llāh (Arabic): literally, "remembrance of God"; in Islam, the recollection of God through various ritual actions; in Sufism, the methodical invocation of a Name or Names of God.

Dīkshā (Sanskrit): in Hinduism, a rite of initiation performed by a *guru*, or spiritual director, and typically involving the gift of a *mantra*, or sacred formula.

Esse (Latin): literally "to be"; the divine Principle as pure Being.

Ex cathedra (Latin): literally, "from the throne"; in Roman Catholicism, authoritative teaching issued by the pope and regarded as infallible.

Ex nihilo (Latin): literally, "out of nothing"; see *creatio ex nihilo*.

Filioque (Latin): "and (from) the Son"; a term added to the Nicene Creed by the Western Church to express the "double procession" of the Holy Spirit from the Father "and the Son"; rejected by the Eastern Orthodox Church.

Gopī (Sanskrit): literally, "keeper of the cows"; in Hindu tradition, one of the cowherd girls involved with Krishna in the love affairs of his youth, symbolic of the soul's devotion to God.

Gratia plena (Latin): literally, "full of grace"; part of the Angelical Salutation, or "Hail Mary" (*Ave Maria*) (cf. Luke 1:28, 42).

Hadīth (Arabic, plural *ahādīth*): "saying, narrative"; an account of the words or deeds of the Prophet Muhammad, transmitted through a traditional chain of known intermediaries.

Hanīf (Arabic): "pure", "upright"; those who, by the purity and uprightness of their nature, practiced the pristine monotheism of Abraham before the coming of Islam, not succumbing to the prevailing polytheism in the Arabian Peninsula.

Haqīqah (Arabic, plural *haqāʾiq*): "truth, reality"; in Sufism, esoteric or metaphysical knowledge of the supremely Real; also the essential reality of a thing.

Hypostasis (Greek, plural *hypostases*): literally, "substance"; the transcendent form of a metaphysical reality, understood to be eternally distinct from all other such forms; in Christian theology, a technical term for one of the three Persons of the Trinity.

Īshvara (Sanskrit): literally, "possessing power", hence master; God understood as a personal being, as Creator and Lord; manifest in the *Trimūrti* as Brahmā, Vishnu, and Shiva.

Ithbāt (Arabic): "affirmation"; the second half of the Islamic testimony of faith, consisting of the two words *illā* and *Allāh*, "if not God".

In divinis (Latin): literally, "in or among divine things"; within the divine Principle; the plural form is used insofar as the Principle comprises dimensions, modes, and degrees.

Jinn (Arabic, singular *jinnī*): genii, or subtle creatures inhabiting the psychic or animic realm, to whom the Koranic message is also addressed.

Jīvan-mukta (Sanskrit): one who is "liberated" while still in this "life"; a person who has attained to a state of spiritual perfection or self-realization before death; in contrast to *videha-mukta*, one who is liberated at the moment of death.

Jnāna or *jnāna-mārga* (Sanskrit): the spiritual "path" (*mārga*) of "knowledge" (*jnāna*) and intellection; see *bhakti* and *karma*.

Karma (Sanskrit): "action, work"; one of the principal *mārgas* or spiritual "paths", characterized by its stress on righteous deeds (see *bhakti* and *jnāna*); in Hinduism and Buddhism, the law of consequence, in which the present is explained by reference to the nature and quality of one's past actions.

Logos (Greek): "word, reason"; in Christian theology, the divine, uncreated Word of God (cf. John 1:1); the transcendent Principle of creation and revelation.

Mahāyāna (Sanskrit): "great vehicle"; the form of Buddhism, including such traditions as Zen and *Jōdo-Shinshū*, which regards itself as the fullest or most adequate expression of the Buddha's teaching; distinguished by the idea that *Nirvāna* is not other than *samsāra* truly seen as it is.

Mater Dei (Latin): literally, "Mother of God"; a title of the Virgin Mary.

Māyā (Sanskrit): universal illusion, relativity, appearance; in *Advaita Vedānta*, the veiling or concealment of *Brahma* in the form or under the appearance of a lower, relative reality; when viewed positively, *Māyā* is also "productive power", the unveiling or manifestation of *Ātmā* as "divine art" or theophany. Neither real nor unreal, it ranges from the supreme Lord to the "last blade of grass".

Modus vivendi (Latin): literally, "mode of living"; a practical compromise or working arrangement between competing interests.

Mūdra (Sanskrit): literally, "seal"; in Hinduism and Buddhism, a symbolical ritual gesture, most often of the hands or fingers.

Mutatis mutandis (Latin): a phrase meaning, "with the necessary changes having been made".

Nafy (Arabic): "negation"; the first half of the Islamic testimony of faith, consisting in the two Arabic words *lā ilāha*, "no god".

Nirvāna (Sanskrit): literally, "blowing out"; in Indian traditions, especially Buddhism, the extinction of suffering and the resulting, supremely blissful state of liberation from egoism and attachment.

Para-Brahma (Sanskrit): the "supreme" or ultimate *Brahma*, also called *Brahma nirguna*; in Schuon's teaching, the "pure Absolute".

Pneuma (Greek): the spirit that predominates over the soul and the body (cf. 1 Thess. 5:23; 1 Cor. 2:14-15).

Pontifex (Latin): literally, "bridge-builder"; in ancient Rome, a member of the council of priests; in Christianity, a bishop; used by the author to refer to sacerdotal man as the intermediary or bridge between Heaven and earth.

Posse (Latin): literally, "to be able"; the divine Principle as infinite Possibility.

Prajnā (Sanskrit): "wisdom, intelligence, understanding"; in Hinduism, the self-awareness of *Ātmā*; liberating knowledge of things as they truly are.

Prakriti (Sanskrit): literally, "making first"; the fundamental, "feminine" substance or material cause of all things; see *Purusha*.

Purusha (Sanskrit): literally, "man"; the informing or shaping principle of creation; the "masculine" demiurge or fashioner of the universe; see *Prakriti*.

Quod absit (Latin): literally, "which thing, let it be absent"; a wish or a command used by the medieval Scholastics to call attention to an idea that is absurdly inconsistent with accepted principles.

Rajas (Sanskrit): in Hinduism, one of the three *gunas*, or qualities, of *Prakriti*, of which all things are woven; the quality of expansiveness, manifest in the material world as force or movement and in the soul as ambition, initiative, and restlessness.

Rishi (Sanskrit): literally, "seer"; in Hinduism the original sages to whom the sacred texts of the *Veda*s were revealed.

Samsāra (Sanskrit): literally, "wandering"; in Hinduism and Buddhism, transmigration or the cycle of birth, death, and rebirth; also the world of apparent flux and change.

Samskāra (Sanskrit): literally, "accomplishment"; a rite of passage in Hinduism, Buddhism, and Jainism.

Sannyāsī (Sanskrit): "renunciate"; in Hinduism, one who has renounced all formal ties to family, caste, and property, in accordance with the fourth stage of life.

Sat (Sanskrit): "being"; one of the three essential aspects of *Apara-Brahma*, together with *Chit*, "consciousness", and *Ānanda*, "bliss, beatitude, joy".

Sattva (Sanskrit): in Hinduism, one of the three *gunas*, or qualities, of *Prakriti*, of which all things are woven; the quality of luminosity, manifest in the material world as buoyancy or lightness and in the soul as intelligence and virtue.

Shahādah (Arabic): the fundamental "profession" or "testimony" of faith in Islam, consisting of the words *Lā ilāha illā 'Llāh, Muhammadan rasūlu 'Llāh*: "There is no god but God; Muhammad is the messenger of God."

Shakti (Sanskrit): creative "power" or radiant "energy"; in Hinduism, expressed tantrically as the divine consort or feminine complement of Shiva.

Shāstra (Sanskrit): literally, "command, rule"; in Hinduism, a collection of precepts concerning important aspects of social and religious life; the best-known example is the *Mānava Dharma Shāstra*, or Law of Manu.

Tamas (Sanskrit): in Hinduism, one of the three *gunas*, or qualities, of *Prakriti*, of which all things are woven; the quality of darkness or heaviness, manifest in the material world as inertia or rigidity and in the soul as sloth, stupidity, and vice.

Tantra (Sanskrit): literally, "warp on a loom"; in Hindu tradition, any of several methods of interiorizing and transforming sensual enjoyment for the sake of a spiritual end.

Tārā (Sanskrit): literally, "she who saves"; the title of a number of Tibetan female *Bodhisattva*s and Hindu goddesses.

Upāya (Sanskrit): "means, expedient, method"; in Buddhist tradition, the adaptation of spiritual teaching to a form suited to the level of one's audience.

Vacare Deo (Latin): literally, "to be empty for God"; to be at leisure or available to God; in the Christian monastic and contemplative tradition, to set aside time from work for meditation and prayer.

Vedānta (Sanskrit): "end or culmination of the *Vedas*"; one of the major schools of traditional Hindu philosophy, based in part on the *Upanishads*, esoteric treatises found at the conclusion of the Vedic scriptures; see *advaita*.

Weltanschauung (German): literally, "view of the world"; a fundamental worldview.

Wu-Yu (Chinese): literally, "non-being"; the supreme *Tao* (*wu-yu*), unconditioned and "without name"; in contradistinction to the non-supreme *Tao* (*yu*), conditioned and "with name".

Yin-Yang (Chinese): in Chinese tradition, two opposite but complementary forces or qualities, from whose interpenetration the universe and all its diverse forms emerge; *yin* corresponds to the feminine, the yielding, the moon, and liquidity; *yang* corresponds to the masculine, the resisting, the sun, and solidity.

For a glossary of all key foreign words used in books published by
World Wisdom, including metaphysical terms in English, consult:
www.DictionaryofSpiritualTerms.org.
This on-line Dictionary of Spiritual Terms provides extensive
definitions, examples, and related terms in other languages.

INDEX

Aaron, 110

Abel, 109, 110

Abraham (patriarch), 107, 110, 124, 158, 171, 179

Absolute, the, 5, 6, 11, 17, 18, 19, 24, 25, 31, 32, 33, 34, 35, 36, 37, 44, 46, 48, 53, 56, 61, 65, 66, 74, 75, 78, 88, 111, 114, 115, 119, 127, 129, 134, 141, 149, 154, 156, 160, 171, 177, 178, 181

Abu Bakr (first Caliph of Islam), 109, 170

Acts of the Apostles, 96

Adam, 84, 162, 163

Advaita Vedānta. See *Vedānta*

Agathon, 31, 146, 177. *See also* Good; Sovereign Good

Alcaeus, 12, 153

Allāh, 45, 46, 110, 157, 159, 180

All-Possibility, 53, 56, 80, 83

American Indians, 101

Amidism, 77, 78, 125, 129, 161, 173

androgyne, primordial 75, 161

angelology, Islamic, 145, 176

anthropology, spiritual, 66

Apala, 78, 162

Apara-Brahma, 42, 135, 177, 178, 182

ape(s), 83, 84, 163

Apocatastasis, 150

Apostles, the, 100, 171

archetype, 14, 37, 39, 43, 51, 76, 79, 129. *See also* Platonic "ideas"

Arianism, 129, 173

aristocracy, 122

Aristotelianism, 107, 169

Aristotle, 20, 24, 62, 154, 158, 160, 163, 165, 169

asceticism, Muslim, 117

Ashari, 19, 154, 157

Ātmā, 24, 41, 46, 58, 60, 74, 77, 78, 80, 129, 135, 149, 178, 180

Augustine, 138, 156, 174

Avatāra(s), 79, 80, 105, 113, 162, 163, 173, 178

Babylonian captivity (of Jews), 102, 167

Basil, 90, 164

Beatitude, 34, 109, 137

Beauty, 59, 70, 73, 88, 141, 142

Being, 22, 26, 34, 40, 42, 43, 45, 47, 48, 49, 60, 65, 75, 80, 82, 87, 135, 138, 140, 143, 144, 146, 148, 149, 154, 155, 157, 165, 174, 179

Beyond-Being, 18, 22, 24, 42, 44, 45, 48, 135, 140, 155, 157, 174. *See also* Essence (divine); Godhead; Non-Being

Bhagavad Gītā, 125, 173

bhakti, 105, 107, 178, 180

Bible, 99, 109, 111, 112, 165

Bliss, 49, 85, 148

Bodhi, 75, 85, 178

Bodhisattva(s), 76, 81, 91, 114, 171, 178, 182

Brahmanism, 102, 105. *See also* Hinduism

Brahmanists, 105

breast, 82

Brihadāranyaka Upanishad, 78, 162

Buddha, the, 76, 91, 102, 105, 113, 161, 168, 172, 180

BIOGRAPHICAL NOTES

FRITHJOF SCHUON

Born in Basle, Switzerland in 1907, Frithjof Schuon was the twentieth century's pre-eminent spokesman for the perennialist school of comparative religious thought.

The leitmotif of Schuon's work was foreshadowed in an encounter during his youth with a marabout who had accompanied some members of his Senegalese village to Basle for the purpose of demonstrating their African culture. When Schuon talked with him, the venerable old man drew a circle with radii on the ground and explained: "God is the center; all paths lead to Him." Until his later years Schuon traveled widely, from India and the Middle East to America, experiencing traditional cultures and establishing lifelong friendships with Hindu, Buddhist, Christian, Muslim, and American Indian spiritual leaders.

A philosopher in the tradition of Plato, Shankara, and Eckhart, Schuon was a gifted artist and poet as well as the author of over twenty books on religion, metaphysics, sacred art, and the spiritual path. Describing his first book, *The Transcendent Unity of Religions*, T. S. Eliot wrote, "I have met with no more impressive work in the comparative study of Oriental and Occidental religion", and world-renowned religion scholar Huston Smith said of Schuon, "The man is a living wonder; intellectually apropos religion, equally in depth and breadth, the paragon of our time". Schuon's books have been translated into over a dozen languages and are respected by academic and religious authorities alike.

More than a scholar and writer, Schuon was a spiritual guide for seekers from a wide variety of religions and backgrounds throughout the world. He died in 1998.

PATRICK LAUDE is a professor of theology at Georgetown University School of Foreign Service in Qatar.

A widely recognized writer on the *sophia perennis* and the perennialist school, Professor Laude is co-author of *Frithjof Schuon (1907-1998): Life and Teachings* and co-editor of *Dossier H: Frithjof Schuon*. His other publications include: *Pathways to an Inner Islam: Massignon, Corbin, Guénon, and Schuon, Pray Without Ceasing: The Way of the Invocation in World Religions, Divine Play, Sacred Laughter, and Spiritual Understanding*, and *Singing the Way: Insights in Poetry and Spiritual Transformation*. Professor Laude has also edited a volume on the *Universal Dimensions of Islam* in World Wisdom's series of Studies in Comparative Religion.